D1500858

Birds of Kentucky

Field Guide

by Stan Tekiela

ADVENTURE PUBLICATIONS, INC.
CAMBRIDGE, MINNESOTA

TO MY WIFE KATHERINE AND DAUGHTER ABIGAIL WITH ALL MY LOVE

ACKNOWLEDGMENTS:

Special thanks to Kentucky birders Brainard Palmer-Ball, Jr. and Gary Ritchison for reviewing the range maps.

Edited by Sandy Livoti

Range maps produced by Anthony Hertzel

Book design and illustrations by Jonathan Norberg

Photo credits by photographer and page number:

Cover photo: Male Northern Cardinal by Maslowski Wildlife Productions
Brian Collins: 2, 120, 160, 214, 220, 230 **Cornell Laboratory of Ornithology**: 58, 60 (female), 194 (both) **Dudley Edmondson**: 14, 16 (soaring), 40 (soaring), 42 (all), 64, 68, 74, 80, 86 (both), 114 (in flight), 126 (both), 128 (male), 134, 140 (soaring), 152 (both), 158, 174 (male), 184, 192 (male), 196 (both), 198, 202, 236, 238, 244 (male, winter male), 246, 252 (male), 258 **Carrol Henderson**: 82 **Kevin T. Karlson**: 34, 132, 250 (female) **Bruce Leventhal**: 240 **Bill Marchel**: 6, 22 (male), 24, 30, 60 (male), 72, 88 (white-striped), 92, 104, 122, 136, 140 (perching), 148, 150, 172, 174 (female), 208, 210 (both), 216, 222, 228 **Maslowski Wildlife Productions**: 20, 50, 62, 66 (soaring), 78, 100, 106, 110, 116, 164, 166, 170, 186, 234, 242, 248, 254, 256, 262 **Steve Mortensen**: 22 (female), 26 (male), 28 (both), 38 (both), 40 (perching), 46, 48, 52, 54 (both), 84, 144, 154, 168, 180, 182, 212, 244 (female), 264 (both) **Warren Nelson**: 10, 26 (female), 128 (female), 192 (female), 252 (female) **John Pennoyer**: 70, 218, 226 **Brian E. Small**: 94, 108 (winter), 138, 176, 224, 232, 250 (male), 260 **Stan Tekiela**: 4, 8, 12, 18 (all), 32 (both), 36, 44, 56 (both), 66 (perching), 76, 88 (tan-striped), 90 (both), 96 (adult, 1 year old), 98, 102, 108 (breeding), 112, 114 (perching), 118 (both), 124, 130, 146, 156, 162 (all), 178, 188, 190 (both), 204, 206, 266 **Brian K. Wheeler**: 16 (perching), 142 (both), 200 (both) **Jim Zipp**: 96 (Bohemian)

To the best of the publisher's knowledge, all photos except the female Indigo Bunting were of live birds.

10 9 8 7 6
Copyright 2001 by Stan Tekiela
Published by Adventure Publications, Inc.
820 Cleveland St. S
Cambridge, MN 55008
1-800-678-7006
www.adventurepublications.net
All rights reserved
Printed in China
ISBN-13: 978-1-885061-96-6
ISBN-10: 1-885061-96-X

TABLE OF CONTENTS
Introduction

Sample Page

The Birds

WHY WATCH BIRDS IN KENTUCKY?

Millions of people have discovered bird feeding. It's a simple and enjoyable way to bring the beauty of birds closer to your home. Watching birds at your feeder often leads to a lifetime pursuit of bird identification. The *Birds of Kentucky Field Guide* is for those who want to identify common birds of Kentucky.

There are over 800 species of birds found in North America. In Kentucky alone there have been more than 360 different kinds of birds recorded through the years. These bird sightings were diligently recorded by hundreds of bird watchers and became part of the official state record. From these valuable records, I have chosen 112 of the most common birds of Kentucky to include in this field guide.

Bird watching, often called birding, is the largest spectator sport in America. Its outstanding popularity in Kentucky is due, in part, to an unusually rich and abundant birdlife. Why are there so many birds? One reason is open space. Kentucky is more than 40,000 square miles (104,000 sq. km), making it the thirty-seventh largest state. Despite its size, only about 4 million people call Kentucky home. On average, that's only 91 people per square mile (35 per sq. km). Most of these people are located in and around only three major cities.

Open space is not the only reason there is such an abundance of birds. It's also the diversity of habitat. The state can be broken into several distinct habitats, each of which supports a different group of birds. Water also plays a big part of Kentucky's bird populations. The Ohio River comprises the entire northern border of the state. The Big Sandy and Tug Fork Rivers form much of the eastern border and the Mississippi River forms the western boundary. All of these riverways provide critical habitats for a wide variety of birds. For example, the floodplain forest along the Mississippi River in western Kentucky is a good place to see wetland birds such as the Belted Kingfisher.

The south central portion of the state (Highland Rim), which was originally a prairie habitat, is now agricultural with many open country birds such as the Horned Lark and Eastern Kingbird.

Eastern Kentucky (Cumberland Plateau and Appalachian Plateau) is known for its extensive tracts of forest, rolling hills and mountain ranges. The forested valleys and ridges are home to many birds such as the Scarlet Tanager.

Varying habitats in Kentucky also mean variations in weather. Since the state extends over 400 miles (644 km) from east to west, the weather ranges greatly. From the high and relatively snowy Appalachian Plateau in the east to the steamy summers in the lowland western Kentucky, there are birds to watch in every season. Whether witnessing a migration of hawks in the fall or welcoming back the hummingbirds in the spring, there is variety and excitement in birding as each season turns to the next.

OBSERVE WITH A STRATEGY; TIPS FOR IDENTIFYING BIRDS

Identifying birds isn't as difficult as you might think. By following a few basic strategies, you can increase your chances of successfully identifying most birds you see! One of the first and easiest things to do when you see a new bird is to note its color. (Also, since this book is organized by color, you will go right to that color section to find it.)

Next, note the size of the bird. A strategy to quickly estimate size is to select a small-, medium- and large-sized bird to use for reference. For example, most people are familiar with robins. A robin, measured from the tip of its bill to the tip of its tail, is 10 inches long. Using the robin as an example of a medium-sized bird, select two other birds, one smaller and one larger. Many people use a House Sparrow, at about 6 inches, and an American Crow, about 18 inches. When you see a bird that you don't know, you can quickly ask yourself, "Is it smaller than a robin, but larger than a sparrow?" When you look in your field guide to help identify your bird, you'll know it's roughly between 6 and 10 inches long. This will help narrow your choices.

Next, note the size, shape and color of the bill. Is it long, thin, pointed, short, thick, blunt, curved or straight? Seed-eating birds, such as Northern Cardinals, have bills that are thick and strong enough to crack even the toughest seeds. Birds that sip nectar, such as Ruby-throated Hummingbirds, need long thin bills to reach deep into flowers. Hawks and owls tear their prey with very sharp, curved bills. Sometimes, just noting the bill shape can help you decide if the bird is a woodpecker, finch, grosbeak or blackbird.

Next, take a look around and note the habitat in which you see the bird. Is it wading in a marsh? Walking along a riverbank? Soaring in the sky? Is it perched high in the trees or hopping along the forest floor? Because of their preferences in diet and habitat, you'll usually see robins hopping on the ground, but not often eating the seeds at your feeder. Or you'll see a Rose-breasted Grosbeak sitting on the branches of a tree, but not climbing down the tree trunk the way a nuthatch does.

Noticing what a bird is eating will give you another clue to help you identify that bird. Feeding is a big part of any bird's life. Fully one-third of all bird activity revolves around searching for and catching food, or actually eating. While birds don't always follow all the rules of what we think they eat, you can make some general assumptions. Northern Flickers, for instance, feed upon ants and other insects, so you wouldn't expect to see them visiting a backyard bird feeder. Some birds, such as the Barn Swallow and the Tree Swallow, feed on flying insects, and spend hours swooping and diving to catch a meal.

Sometimes you can identify a bird by the way it perches. Body posture can help you differentiate between an American Crow and a Red-tailed Hawk. American Crows lean forward over their feet on a branch, while hawks perch in a vertical position. Look for this the next time you see a large unidentified bird in a tree.

Birds in flight are often difficult to identify, but noting the size and shape of the wing will help. A bird's wing size is in direct proportion to its body size, weight and type of flying. The shape of the wing determines if the bird flies fast and with precision, or slowly and less precisely. Birds such as House Finches, which flit around in thick tangles of branches, have short round wings. Birds that soar on warm updrafts of air, such as Turkey Vultures, have long broad wings. Barn Swallows have short pointed wings that slice through air, propelling their swift and accurate flight.

Some birds have unique flight patterns that aid in identification. American Goldfinches fly in a distinctive up-and-down pattern that makes it look as if they are riding a roller coaster.

While it's not easy to make these observations in the short time you often have to watch a "mystery bird," practicing these methods of identification will greatly expand your skills in birding. Also, seek the guidance of a more experienced birder who will help you improve your skills and answer questions on the spot.

BIRD BASICS

It's easier to identify birds and communicate about them if you know the names of the different parts of a bird. For instance, it's much easier to use the word "crest" to describe the erect feathers on the head of a Northern Cardinal than trying to describe it.

The following illustration points out the basic parts of a bird. Because it's a composite of many birds, it should not be confused with any actual bird.

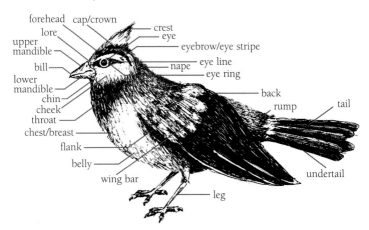

BIRD COLOR VARIABLES

No other animal has a color pallet like a bird's. Vivid blues, lemon yellows, intense reds and iridescent greens are commonplace within the bird world. In general, male birds are more colorful than their female counterparts. This is probably to help the male attract a mate, essentially saying, "Hey, look at me!" It also calls attention to the male's overall health. The better the condition of his feathers, the better his food source and territory, and therefore, the better his potential for a mate.

Female birds that don't look like their male counterparts (such species are called sexually dimorphic, meaning "two forms") are often a nondescript brown color, as seen with Rose-breasted Grosbeaks. These muted tones help to hide the females during weeks of motionless incubation, and draw less attention to her when she is out feeding or taking a break from the rigors of raising her young.

In some species, such as the Bald Eagle, Blue Jay and Downy Woodpecker, the male birds look nearly identical to the females. In the case of the woodpeckers, the sexes are only differentiated by a single red or sometimes yellow mark. Depending on the species, the mark may be on top of the head, face, nape of the neck or just behind the bill.

During the first year, juvenile birds often look like the mothers. Since brightly colored feathers are used mainly for attracting a mate, young non-breeding males don't have a need for colorful plumage. It is not until the first spring molt (or several years later, depending on the species) that young males obtain their breeding colors.

Both breeding and winter plumages are the result of molting. Molting is the process of dropping old worn feathers and replacing them with new ones. All birds molt, typically twice a year, with the spring molt usually occurring in late winter. During this time, most birds produce their breeding plumage (brighter colors for attracting mates), which lasts throughout the summer.

Winter plumage is the result of the late summer molt, which serves a couple of important functions. First, it adds feathers for warmth in the coming winter. Second, in some species it produces feathers that tend to be drab in color, which helps to camouflage the birds and hide them from predators. The winter plumage of the male American Goldfinch, for example, is an olive brown, unlike its obvious canary yellow color in summer. Luckily for us, some birds, such as the male Northern Cardinal, retain their bright summer colors all year long.

BIRD NESTS

Bird nests are truly an amazing feat of engineering. Imagine building your home strong enough to weather a storm, large enough to hold your entire family, insulated enough to shelter them from cold and heat, and waterproof enough to keep out rain. Now, build it without any blueprints or directions, and without the use of your hands or feet! Birds do!

Before building a nest, an appropriate site must be selected. With some birds, such as the House Wren, the male picks out several potential sites and assembles several small twigs in each. This discourages other birds from using nearby nest cavities. These "extra" nests are sometimes called dummy nests. The female is then taken around and shown all the choices. She chooses her favorite and finishes constructing the nest. With some other species of birds, for example, Baltimore Orioles, it's the female who chooses the site and builds the nest with the male only offering an occasional suggestion. Each bird species has its own nest-building routine, which is strictly followed.

Nesting material usually consists of natural elements found in the immediate area. Most nests consist of plant fibers (such as bark peeled from grapevines), sticks, mud, dried grass, feathers, fur, or soft fuzzy tufts from thistle. Some birds, including Ruby-throated Hummingbirds, use spider webs to glue nest materials together. Nesting material is limited to what a bird can hold or carry. Because of this, a bird must make many trips afield to gather enough materials to complete its nest. Most nests take at least four days or more, and hundreds, if not thousands, of trips to build.

As you'll see in the following illustrations, birds build a wide variety of nest types.

| **ground nest** | **platform nest** | **cup nest** | **pendulous nest** | **cavity nest** |

The simple **ground nest** is scraped out of earth. These shallow depressions usually contain no nesting material, and are made by birds such as the Killdeer and Horned Lark.

Another kind of nest, the **platform nest**, represents a more complex type of nest building. Constructed of small twigs and branches, the platform nest is a simple arrangement of sticks which forms a platform and features a small depression to nestle the eggs.

Some platform nests, such as those of the Canada Goose, are constructed on the ground, and are made of mud and grass. Platform nests can also be on cliffs, bridges, balconies or even in flowerpots. This kind of nest gives space to adventurous youngsters, and functions as a landing platform for the parents. Many waterfowl construct platform nests on the ground, usually near water or actually in the water. These floating platform nests vary with the water level, thus preventing nests with eggs from being flooded. Platform nests, constructed by such birds as Mourning Doves and herons, are not anchored to the tree, and may tumble from the branches during high winds and storms.

The **cup nest** is a modified platform nest, used by three-quarters of all songbirds. Constructed from the outside in, a supporting platform is constructed first. This platform is attached firmly to a tree, shrub, rock ledge or the ground. Next, the sides are constructed of grasses, small twigs, bark or leaves, which are woven together and often glued with mud for additional strength. The inner cup, lined with feathers, animal fur, soft plant material or animal hair, is constructed last. The mother bird uses her chest to cast the final contours of the inner nest.

The **pendulous nest** is an unusual nest, looking more like a sock hanging from a branch than a nest. Inaccessible to most predators, these nests are attached to the ends of the smallest branches of a tree, and often wave wildly in the breeze. Woven very tightly of plant fibers, they are strong and watertight, taking up to a week to build. More commonly used by tropical birds, this complicated nest type has also been mastered by orioles and kinglets. A small opening on the top or side allows the parents access to the grass-lined interior. (It must be one heck of a ride to be inside one of these nests during a windy spring thunderstorm!)

Another nest type, the **cavity nest**, is used by many birds, including woodpeckers and Eastern Bluebirds. The cavity nest is usually excavated in a tree branch or trunk, and offers shelter from storms, sun, predators and cold spring mornings. A relatively small entrance hole in a tree leads to an inner chamber up to 10 inches below. Usually constructed by woodpeckers, the cavity nest is used only once by its builder, but subsequently can be used for many years by birds such as Wood Ducks, mergansers and bluebirds, which do not have the capability of excavating one for themselves. Kingfishers, on the other hand, excavate a tunnel up to 4 feet long, which connects the entrance in a riverbank to the nest chamber. These cavity nests are often sparsely lined because they are already well insulated.

Some birds, including some swallows, take nest building one step further. They use a collection of small balls of mud to construct an adobe-style home. Constructed under the eaves of houses, under bridges or inside chimneys, some of these nests look like simple cup nests. Others are completely enclosed, with small tunnel-like openings that lead into a safe nesting chamber for the baby birds.

One of the most clever of all nest types is known as the **no nest** or daycare nest. Parasitic birds, such as Brown-headed Cowbirds, build no nests at all! The egg-laden female expertly searches out other birds' nests and sneaks in to lay one of her own eggs while the host mother is not looking, thereby leaving the host mother to raise an adopted youngster. The mother cowbird wastes no energy building a nest only to have it raided by a predator. By using several nests of other birds, she spreads out her progeny in hope that at least one of her offspring will live to maturity.

WHO BUILDS THE NEST?

In general, the female bird builds the nest. She gathers nesting materials and constructs a nest, with an occasional visit from her mate to check on the progress. In some species, both parents contribute equally to the construction of a nest. A male bird might forage for precisely the right sticks, grass or mud, but it's often the female that forms or puts together the nest. She uses her body to form the egg chamber. Rarely does the male build a nest by himself.

FLEDGING

Fledging is the interval between hatching and flight or leaving the nest. Some birds leave the nest within hours of hatching (precocial), but it might be weeks before they are able to fly. This is common with waterfowl and shorebirds. Until they start to fly, they are called fledglings. Birds that are still in the nest are called nestlings. Other baby birds are born naked and blind, and remain in the nest for several weeks (altricial).

WHY BIRDS MIGRATE

Why do birds migrate? The short answer is simple–food. Birds migrate to areas of high food concentrations. It is easier to breed where food is than where it is not. A typical migrating bird, the Rose-breasted Grosbeak, for instance, migrates from the tropics of Central and South America to nest in the forests of North America, taking advantage of billions of newly hatched insects to feed its young. This trip is called **complete migration**.

Some birds of prey return from their complete migration to northern regions that are overflowing with small rodents, such as mice and voles, that have continued to breed in winter.

Complete migrators have a set time and pattern of migration. Each year at nearly the same time, they take off and head for a specific wintering ground. Complete migrators may travel incredible distances, sometimes as much as 15,000 miles or more in one year. But complete migration doesn't necessarily imply flying from the cold and frozen northland to some tropical destination. Dark-eyed Junco, for example, is a complete migrator that flies from the far reaches of Canada to spend the winter right here in Kentucky.

There are many interesting aspects to complete migrators. In the spring, males usually migrate several weeks before the females, arriving early to scope out possible nesting sites and food sources, and to begin to defend territories. The females arrive several weeks later. In the autumn, in many species, the females and their young leave early, often up to four weeks before the adult males.

Not all migrators are the same. There are **partial migrators**, such as American Goldfinches, that usually wait until food supplies dwindle before they fly south. Unlike complete migrators, the partial migrators move only far enough south, or sometimes east and west, to find abundant food. Some years it might be only a few hundred miles, while other years it might be nearly a thousand. This kind of migration, dependent upon the weather and available food, is sometimes called **seasonal movement**.

Unlike the predictable ebbing and flowing behavior of complete migrators or partial migrators, **irruptive migrators** can move every third to fifth year, or in some cases, in consecutive years. These migrations are triggered when times are really tough and food is scarce. Red-breasted Nuthatches are a good example of irruptive migrators, because they leave their normal northern range in search of food or in response to overpopulation.

How Do Birds Migrate?

One of the many secrets of migration is fat. While we humans are fighting the battle of the bulge, birds intentionally gorge themselves to put on as much fat as possible while still being able to fly. Fat provides the greatest amount of energy per unit of weight, and in the same way that your car needs gas, birds are propelled by fat or stalled without it.

During long migratory flights, fat deposits are used up quickly, and birds need to stop to "refuel." This is when backyard bird feeding stations and undeveloped, natural spaces around our towns and cities are especially important. Some birds require up to two to three days of constant feeding to build up their fat reserves before continuing their seasonal trip.

Some birds, such as most eagles, hawks, ospreys, falcons and vultures, migrate during the day. Larger birds can hold more body fat, go longer without eating and take longer to migrate. These birds glide along on rising columns of warm air, called thermals, which hold them aloft while they slowly make their way north or south. They generally rest at night and hunt early in the morning before the sun has a chance to warm up the land and create good soaring conditions. Birds migrating during the day use a combination of landforms, rivers, and the rising and setting sun to guide them in the right direction.

Most other birds migrate during the night. Studies show that some birds which migrate at night use the stars to navigate. Others use the setting sun, while still others, such as doves, use the earth's magnetic fields to guide them north or south. While flying at night might seem like a crazy idea, nocturnal migration is safer for several reasons. First, there are fewer nighttime predators for migrating birds. Second, traveling at night allows time during the day to find food in unfamiliar surroundings. Finally, nighttime wind patterns tend to be flat, or laminar. These flat winds don't have the turbulence associated with the daytime winds, and can actually help carry smaller birds by pushing them along.

HOW TO USE THIS GUIDE

To help you quickly and easily identify birds, this book is organized by color. Simply note the color of the bird and turn to that section. Refer to the first page for the color key. The male Rose-breasted Grosbeak, for example, is black-and-white with a red patch on its chest. Because the bird is mostly black and white, it will be found in the black and white section. Each color section is also arranged by size, generally with the smaller birds first. Sections may also incorporate the average size in a range, which in some cases reflects size differences between male and female birds. Flip through the pages in that color section to find the bird. If you already know the name of the bird, check the index for the page number. In some species, the male and female are remarkably different in color. In these cases, the opposite sex is shown in a smaller inset photograph with a page reference. These birds, therefore, will be found in two different color sections.

In the description section you will find a variety of information about the bird. On the next page is a sample of the information included in the book.

RANGE MAPS

Range maps are included for each bird. Colored areas indicate where in Kentucky a particular bird is most likely to be found. The colors represent the presence of a species during a specific season, not the density or amount of birds in the area. Green is used for summer, blue for winter, red for year-round and yellow for areas where the bird is seen during migration. While every effort has been made to accurately depict these ranges, they are only general guidelines. Ranges actually change on an ongoing basis due to a variety of factors. Changes in weather, species abundance, landscape and vital resources such as the availability of food and water can affect local populations, migration and movements, causing birds to be found in areas not typical for the species.

Colored areas simply mean bird sightings for that species have been frequent in those areas and less frequent in the others. Please use the maps as intended–as general guides only.

YEAR-ROUND
MIGRATION
SUMMER
WINTER

RANGE MAP

Size: measures head to tail, may include wingspan

Male: a brief description of the male bird, and may include breeding, winter or other plumages

Female: a brief description of the female bird, which is sometimes not the same as the male

Juvenile: a brief description of the juvenile bird, which often looks like the female

Nest: the kind of nest this bird builds to raise its young, who builds the nest, and how many broods per year

Eggs: how many eggs you might expect to see in a nest, and the color of the eggs

Incubation: the average time the parents spend incubating the eggs, and who does the incubation

Fledging: the average time the young spend in the nest after hatching but before they leave the nest, and which parent(s) does most of the "childcare" and feeding

Migration: type of migration: complete (consistent, seasonal), or partial (seasonal, destination varies), or irruptive (unpredictable, depending on the food supply), or non-migrator

Food: what the bird eats most of the time (e.g., seeds, nectar, insects, fruit, small animals), and if it typically comes to a bird feeding station

Compare: notes about other birds that look similar, and the pages on which they can be found

Stan's Notes: Interesting gee-whiz natural history information. This could be something to look or listen for, or something to help positively identify the bird. Also includes remarkable features.

female
pg. 101

male

EASTERN TOWHEE
Pipilo erythrophthalmus

YEAR-ROUND

Size: 7-8" (18-20 cm)

Male: A mostly black bird with dirty-red-brown sides and white belly. Long black tail with white tip. Short, stout, pointed bill and rich red eyes. White wing patches flash in flight.

Female: similar to male, but is brown, not black

Juvenile: light brown, a heavily streaked head, chest and belly, long dark tail with white tip

Nest: cup; female builds; 2 broods per year

Eggs: 3-4; creamy white with brown markings

Incubation: 12-13 days; female incubates

Fledging: 10-12 days; female and male feed young

Migration: complete, to southern states and South America

Food: insects, seeds, fruit, visits ground feeders

Compare: Slightly smaller than the American Robin (pg. 193). The Gray Catbird (pg. 189) lacks a black "hood" and rusty sides. Common Grackle (pg. 11) lacks white belly and has long thin bill. Male Rose-breasted Grosbeak (pg. 25) has a rosy patch in center of chest.

Stan's Notes: Common name comes from its distinctive "tow-hee" call given by both sexes. Mostly known for its characteristic call that sounds like, "Drink-your-tea!" Seen hopping backward with both feet to rake up leaf litter (bilateral scratching), in search of insects and seeds. The female broods, but male does most of the feeding of young. White-eyed form in southern states, red-eyed elsewhere.

3

female
pg. 99

male

BROWN-HEADED COWBIRD
Molothrus ater

Size: 7½" (19 cm)

Male: A glossy black bird, reminiscent of a Red-winged Blackbird. Chocolate brown head with a pointed, sharp gray bill.

Female: dull brown bird with bill similar to male

Juvenile: similar to female, only dull gray color and a streaked chest

Nest: no nest; lays eggs in nests of other birds

Eggs: 5-7; white with brown markings

Incubation: 10-13 days; host bird incubates eggs

Fledging: 10-11 days; host birds feed young

Migration: complete, to southern states

Food: insects, seeds, will come to seed feeders

Compare: In the blackbird family. The slightly larger male Red-winged Blackbird (pg. 9) has red and yellow markings on wings. Common Grackle (pg. 11) has a long tail and lacks the brown head. European Starling (pg. 7) has yellow bill and shorter tail.

Stan's Notes: Of about 750 species of parasitic birds worldwide, this is the only parasitic bird in Kentucky, laying all eggs in host birds' nests, leaving others to raise its young. Cowbirds are known to have laid eggs in nests of over 200 species of birds. Some birds reject cowbird eggs, but most raise them, even to the exclusion of their own young. Look for warblers and other birds feeding young birds twice their own size. At one time cowbirds followed bison to feed on the insects attracted to the animals.

EUROPEAN STARLING
Sturnus vulgaris

YEAR-ROUND

Size: 7½" (19 cm)

Male: Iridescent purple black bird covered with white speckles during autumn and winter. Shiny purple black in spring and summer. Long, pointed yellow bill in the spring and gray in autumn. Short tail.

Female: same as male

Juvenile: similar to adult, only a gray brown with a streaked chest

Nest: cavity; male and female line the cavity; 2 broods per year

Eggs: 4-6; bluish with brown markings

Incubation: 12-14 days; female and male incubate

Fledging: 18-20 days; female and male feed young

Migration: non-migrator to partial migrator, some will move to southern states

Food: insects, seeds, fruit, comes to seed and suet feeders

Compare: Looks similar to Common Grackle (pg. 11), but lacks its long tail.

Stan's Notes: A great songster, it is also able to mimic sounds. Often displaces woodpeckers, chickadees and other cavity-nesting birds. Can be very aggressive and destroy eggs or young of other birds. The bill changes color with the seasons: yellow in spring and gray in autumn. Jaws are designed to be the most powerful when opening, as they pry open crevices to locate hidden insects. Gathers in the hundreds in autumn. Not a native bird, it was introduced to New York City in 1890-91 from Europe.

female
pg. 113

male

RED-WINGED BLACKBIRD
Agelaius phoeniceus

YEAR-ROUND

Size: 8½" (22 cm)

Male: Jet black bird with red and yellow shoulder patches on upper wings. Pointed black bill.

Female: heavily streaked brown bird with a pointed brown bill and white eyebrows

Juvenile: same as female

Nest: cup; female builds; 2-3 broods per year

Eggs: 3-4; bluish green with brown markings

Incubation: 10-12 days; female incubates

Fledging: 11-14 days; female and male feed young

Migration: complete, to southern states, Mexico and Central America

Food: seeds, insects, will come to seed feeders

Compare: Slightly larger than the male Brown-headed Cowbird (pg. 5), but is less iridescent and lacks Cowbird's brown head. Differs from all blackbirds due to the red and yellow patches on its wings (epaulets).

Stan's Notes: One of the most widespread and numerous birds in Kentucky. It is a sure sign of spring when Red-winged Blackbirds return to the marshes. Flocks of up to 100,000 birds have been reported. Males return before the females and defend territories by singing from the tops of surrounding vegetation. Will repeat call from top of cattail while showing off its red and yellow wing bars (epaulets). Nests are usually over shallow water in thick stands of cattails. They feed mostly on seeds in spring and fall, switching to insects during summer. Females choose mate.

COMMON GRACKLE
Quiscalus quiscula

YEAR-ROUND

Size:	11-13" (28-33 cm)
Male:	Large black bird with iridescent blue black head, purple brown body, long black tail, long thin bill and bright golden eyes.
Female:	similar to male, only duller and smaller
Juvenile:	similar to female
Nest:	cup; female builds; 2 broods per year
Eggs:	4-5; greenish white with brown markings
Incubation:	13-14 days; female incubates
Fledging:	16-20 days; female and male feed young
Migration:	complete, to southern states
Food:	fruit, seeds, insects, comes to seed feeders
Compare:	European Starling (pg. 7) is much smaller and has a speckled appearance and yellow bill. Male Red-winged Blackbird (pg. 9) has red and yellow wing markings.

Stan's Notes: Usually nests in small colonies of up to 75 pairs, but travels with other blackbirds in large flocks. Is known to feed in farmers' fields. Name comes from the Latin word *graculus*, meaning "to cough," for its loud raspy call. Male holds tail in a vertical keel-like position during flight. The flight pattern is almost always level, as opposed to having undulating up-and-down movements. Unlike most birds, has larger muscles to open mouth rather than to close it, as it pries open crevices to locate hidden insects.

AMERICAN COOT
Fulica americana

MIGRATION
WINTER

Size: 13-16" (33-40 cm)

Male: Slate gray to black all over, white bill with dark band near tip. Green legs and feet. A small white patch near the base of the tail. Prominent red eyes and a small red patch above bill between eyes.

Female: same as male

Juvenile: much paler than adult, with a gray bill and same white rump patch

Nest: cup; female and male build; 1 brood per year

Eggs: 9-12; pinkish buff with brown markings

Incubation: 21-25 days; female and male incubate

Fledging: 49-52 days; female and male feed young

Migration: complete, to southern states and Central America

Food: insects, aquatic plants

Compare: Smaller than most waterfowl, it is the only black water bird or duck-like bird with a white bill.

Stan's Notes: An excellent diver and swimmer, often seen in large flocks on open water. Not a duck, as it doesn't have webbed feet, but instead has large lobed toes. Look for it to bob its head while swimming. When taking off, it scrambles across the surface of the water with wings flapping. Huge flocks of up to 1,000 birds gather for autumn migration. The unusual name is of unknown origin, but in Middle English, *coote* was used to describe various waterfowl–perhaps it stuck. Floating nests are anchored to vegetation.

13

AMERICAN CROW
Corvus brachyrhynchos

YEAR-ROUND

Size: 18" (45 cm)

Male: All-black bird with black bill, legs and feet. Can have purple sheen in direct sunlight.

Female: same as male

Juvenile: same as adult

Nest: platform; female builds; 1 brood per year

Eggs: 4-6; bluish to olive green, brown markings

Incubation: 18 days; female incubates

Fledging: 28-35 days; female and male feed young

Migration: non-migrator to partial migrator

Food: fruit, insects, mammals, fish, carrion, will come to seed and suet feeders

Compare: Similar to the Common Raven (rarely seen in Kentucky), but has smaller bill and lacks shaggy throat feathers. Crow has a higher pitched call than Raven's deep, low raspy call. Crow has a squared tail. Raven has a wedge-shaped tail, apparent in flight.

Stan's Notes: One of the most recognizable birds in Kentucky. Often reuses nest every year if not taken over by a Great Horned Owl. Collects and stores bright, shiny objects in the nest. Able to mimic human voices, and other birds. One of the smartest of all birds, it is very social, often entertaining itself by provoking chases with other birds. Feeds on road kill but is rarely hit by cars. Can live up to 20 years. Unmated birds, known as helpers, help raise young. Large extended families roost together at night, dispersing during the day to hunt.

soaring

TURKEY VULTURE
Cathartes aura

SUMMER

Size: 26-32" (66-80 cm); up to 6-foot wingspan

Male: Large bird with obvious red head and legs. In flight, the wings appear two-toned: black leading edge with gray on the trailing edge and tip. The tips of wings end in finger-like projections. Squared-off tail. Ivory bill.

Female: same as male

Juvenile: same as adult, but often a gray-to-blackish head and bill

Nest: no nest, or minimal nest on cliff or in cave; 1 brood per year

Eggs: 2; white with brown markings

Incubation: 38-41 days; female and male incubate

Fledging: 66-88 days; female and male feed young

Migration: complete, to southern states, Central and South America

Food: carrion, just about any dead animal of any size, parents regurgitate for young

Compare: Smaller than the Bald Eagle (pg. 43), look for Vulture's two-toned wings. Flies holding wings in a slight V shape, unlike the Eagle's straight wing position.

Stan's Notes: The Vulture's naked head is an adaptation to reduce the risk of feather fouling (picking up diseases) from carcasses. Unlike hawks and eagles, it has weak feet more suited to walking than grasping. One of the few birds with a developed sense of smell. Generally mute, it makes only grunts or groans. Groups often seen in trees with wings outstretched to catch sun.

17

in flight

juvenile

drying

DOUBLE-CRESTED CORMORANT
Phalacrocorax auritus

Size: 33" (84 cm)

Male: Large black water bird with a long snake-like neck. Two crests on head. Long gray bill with yellow at the base and a hooked tip.

Female: same as male

Juvenile: lighter brown with a grayish-colored breast and neck

Nest: platform, in colony; male and female build; 1 brood per year

Eggs: 3-4; bluish white, unmarked

Incubation: 25-29 days; female and male incubate

Fledging: 37-42 days; male and female feed young

Migration: complete, to southern states, Mexico and Central America

Food: small fish, aquatic insects

Compare: Similar size as the Turkey Vulture (pg. 17), which also perches on branches with wings open to dry in sun, but lacks the Vulture's naked red head. Twice the size of American Coot (pg. 13), which lacks the Cormorant's long neck and long pointed bill.

Stan's Notes: Often seen flying in large V formation. Often roosts in large groups in trees near water. Catches fish by swimming with wings held at its sides. To dry off it strikes an erect pose with wings outstretched, facing the sun. Common name refers to the two crests on its head, which are not usually seen. "Cormorant" comes from the Latin *corvus*, meaning "crow," and *L. marinus*, meaning "pertaining to the sea," literally, "Sea Crow."

BLACK-AND-WHITE WARBLER
Mniotilta varia

Size: 5" (13 cm)

Male: Striped like a zebra, this small warbler has a distinctive black-and-white striped cap. White belly. Black chin and cheek patch.

Female: same as male, only duller and without the black chin and cheek patch

Juvenile: similar to female

Nest: cup; female builds; 1 brood per year

Eggs: 4-5; white with brown markings

Incubation: 10-11 days; female incubates

Fledging: 9-12 days; female and male feed young

Migration: complete, to Central and South America

Food: insects

Compare: Look for Black-and-white Warbler creeping down a tree trunk, like the White-breasted Nuthatch (pg. 173). The Brown Creeper (pg. 65) is brown and white with a white chest and belly. Creeper's bill is longer and curved downward.

Stan's Notes: One of the first warblers to return each spring, it is the only warbler that moves headfirst down a tree trunk. Look for this common warbler searching for insect eggs in the bark of large trees. Female will perform a distraction dance to draw predators away from nest. Makes nest on the ground, concealed under dead leaves or at the base of a tree. Song sounds like a slowly turning, squeaky wheel.

male

female

DOWNY WOODPECKER
Picoides pubescens

Size: 6" (15 cm)

Male: A small woodpecker with an all-white belly, black-and-white spotted wings, a black line running through its eyes, a short black bill, a white stripe down back and a red mark on nape of neck. Several small black spots along side of white tail.

Female: same as male, lacking red mark on nape

Juvenile: same as female, some juveniles can have a red mark near forehead

Nest: cavity; male and female excavate; 1 brood per year

Eggs: 3-5; white, unmarked

Incubation: 11-12 days; female and male incubate, the female during day, male at night

Fledging: 20-25 days; male and female feed young

Migration: non-migrator

Food: insects, seeds, visits seed and suet feeders

Compare: Almost identical to the Hairy Woodpecker (pg. 29), but smaller. Look for the shorter, thinner bill of Downy to differentiate them.

Stan's Notes: One of the most abundant and widespread woodpeckers in Kentucky. Both sexes will drum on a hollow log or a branch to announce territories. Males perform most brooding and incubate all night. Small percentage of young will have a red spot on crown. Stiff tail feathers help brace the bird like a tripod as it clings to a tree branch. All woodpeckers have long barbed tongues, used to pull insects out of tiny places. Will winter roost in cavity.

female
pg. 105

male

ROSE-BREASTED GROSBEAK
Pheucticus ludovicianus

Size: 7-8" (18-20 cm)

Male: A plump black-and-white bird with a large, triangular rose patch in the center of chest. Wing linings are rosy red. Large ivory bill.

Female: heavily streaked brown and white bird with large white eyebrows, orange yellow wing linings

Juvenile: same as female

Nest: cup; the female and male build; 1-2 broods per year

Eggs: 3-5; blue green with brown markings

Incubation: 13-14 days; female and male incubate

Fledging: 9-12 days; female and male feed young

Migration: complete, to Mexico, Central America and South America

Food: insects, seeds, fruit, comes to seed feeders

Compare: Male is very distinctive with no look-alikes.

Stan's Notes: Both male and female sing, but the male sings much louder and clearer. A rich, robin-like song. "Grosbeak" refers to its large bill, used to crush seeds. Male's red breast patch varies in size and shape in each individual. Males arrive first in spring, joined by females several days later. Late to arrive in spring and early to leave in autumn. Often prefers mature deciduous forest for nesting.

male

female

YELLOW-BELLIED SAPSUCKER
Sphyrapicus varius

WINTER

Size: 8-9" (20-22.5 cm)

Male: Medium-sized woodpecker with checkered back. Has a red forehead, crown and chin. Tan-to-yellow chest and belly. White wing patches flash while flying.

Female: similar to male, white marking on chin

Juvenile: similar to adult, dull brown and lacks any red marking

Nest: cavity; female and male excavate; 1 brood per year

Eggs: 5-6; white, unmarked

Incubation: 12-13 days; female and male incubate, the female during day, male at night

Fledging: 25-29 days; female and male feed young

Migration: complete, to Mexico and Central America

Food: insects, tree sap

Compare: Similar to other woodpeckers, but the male is the only Kentucky woodpecker with a red chin patch. Female has white chin.

Stan's Notes: Drills holes in a pattern of horizontal rows in small- to medium-sized trees to bleed tree sap. Many birds drink from sapsucker taps. Oozing sap also attracts insects, which sapsuckers eat. Sapsuckers will defend their sapping sites from other birds. They don't suck sap; rather, they lap it with their long tongues. A quiet bird with few vocalizations, but will mew like a cat. Unlike other woodpeckers, drumming rhythm is irregular.

male

female

HAIRY WOODPECKER
Picoides villosus

YEAR-ROUND

Size: 9" (22.5 cm)

Male: Black-and-white woodpecker with a white belly and black wings with rows of white spots. White stripe down back. Long black bill. Red mark on back of head.

Female: same as male, lacks red spot

Juvenile: grayer version of adult, lacks red spot

Nest: cavity; female and male excavate; 1 brood per year

Eggs: 3-6; white, unmarked

Incubation: 11-15 days; female and male incubate, the female during day, male at night

Fledging: 28-30 days; male and female feed young

Migration: non-migrator

Food: insects, nuts, seeds, comes to seed and suet feeders

Compare: Larger than Downy Woodpecker (pg. 23), Hairy has a longer bill and lacks Downy's black spots along tail.

Stan's Notes: A common backyard bird that announces its arrival with a sharp chirp before landing on feeders. Barbed tongue helps extract insects from trees. Responsible for eating many destructive forest insects. Has tiny bristle-like feathers at base of bill to protect nostrils from wood dust. Will drum on hollow logs, branches or stovepipes in spring to announce territory. Often prefers to excavate nest cavities in live aspen trees. Has a larger, more oval-shaped cavity entrance than that of Downy Woodpecker.

RED-HEADED WOODPECKER
Melanerpes erythrocephalus

YEAR-ROUND
MIGRATION

Size: 9" (22.5 cm)

Male: All-red head and a solid black back. White rump, chest and belly. Large white patches on wings flash when in flight. A black tail. Gray legs and bill.

Female: same as male

Juvenile: gray brown with white chest, lacks any red

Nest: cavity; male builds with help from female; 1 brood per year

Eggs: 4-5; white, unmarked

Incubation: 12-13 days; female and male incubate

Fledging: 27-30 days; female and male feed young

Migration: partial migrator, will move around to areas with abundant supply of nuts

Food: insects, nuts, fruit, comes to seed and suet feeders

Compare: No other Kentucky woodpecker has an all-red head. Pileated Woodpecker (pg. 39) is the only other woodpecker that has a solid black back, but has a partial red head.

Stan's Notes: One of the few woodpecker species in which male and female appear the same (look alike). Bill is not as well adapted for excavating holes as in other woodpeckers, so it chooses dead or rotten tree branches for nest. Later nesting than the closely related Red-bellied Woodpecker and will often take over its nesting cavity. Prefers more open or edge woodland with many dead trees. Often seen perching on tops of dead snags. Stores acorns and other nuts.

male

female

RED-BELLIED WOODPECKER
Melanerpes carolinus

Size: 9¼" (23 cm)

Male: "Zebra-backed" woodpecker with a white rump. Red crown extends down the nape of neck. Tan breast with a tinge of red on belly, which is often hard to see.

Female: same as male, but gray crown

Juvenile: gray version of adult, no red crown or nape

Nest: cavity; the female and male build; 1 brood per year

Eggs: 4-5; white, unmarked

Incubation: 12-14 days; female and male incubate, the female during day, male at night

Fledging: 24-27 days; female and male feed young

Migration: non-migrator

Food: insects, nuts, fruit, comes to seed and suet feeders

Compare: Similar to Northern Flicker (pg. 129) and Yellow-bellied Sapsucker (pg. 27). Note the tan chest and belly with obvious black-and-white stripes on back. The Red-headed Woodpecker (pg. 31) has an all-red head.

Stan's Notes: Named for its easily overlooked rosy-red belly patch. Mostly a bird of shady woodland, it excavates holes in rotten wood looking for spiders, centipedes and beetles. Hammers acorns and berries into crevices of trees for winter food. Will return to same tree to excavate a new nest below that of the previous year. Often kicked out of nest hole by European Starlings.

female pg. 139

male

LESSER SCAUP
Aythya affinis

MIGRATION
WINTER

Size: 16-17" (40-43 cm)

Male: Appears mostly black with bold white sides and gray back. Chest and head look nearly black, but head appears purple with green highlights in direct sun. Bright yellow eyes.

Female: overall brown with dull white patch at base of light-gray bill, yellow eyes

Juvenile: same as female

Nest: ground; female builds; 1 brood per year

Eggs: 8-14; olive buff without markings

Incubation: 22-28 days; female incubates

Fledging: 45-50 days; female teaches young to feed

Migration: complete, southern states, northern South America, Central America

Food: aquatic plants and insects

Compare: Male Blue-winged Teal (pg. 137) is smaller and has bright white crescent-shaped patch near base of bill.

Stan's Notes: A common diving duck in Kentucky. Often seen in large flocks on area lakes, ponds and sewage lagoons. Usually only seen during spring and fall migrations. When observed in flight, note the bold white stripe under the wings. Interesting baby-sitting arrangement in which the young form groups tended by one to three adult females.

female pg. 147

male

HOODED MERGANSER
Lophodytes cucullatus

Size: 16-19" (40-48 cm)

Male: A sleek black-and-white bird with rusty brown sides. Crest "hood" raises to reveal large white patch. Long, thin black bill.

Female: sleek brown and rust bird with a ragged rusty crest and long, thin brown bill

Juvenile: similar to female

Nest: cavity; female lines old woodpecker hole; 1 brood per year

Eggs: 10-12; white, unmarked

Incubation: 32-33 days; female incubates

Fledging: 71 days; female feeds young

Migration: complete, to Gulf coast and Mexico

Food: small fish, aquatic insects

Compare: A distinctive diving bird, look for the large white patch on the head and rusty sides. Similar size as the male Wood Duck (pg. 213), but lacking the green head of the Wood Duck.

Stan's Notes: A small diving bird of shallow-water ponds, sloughs, lakes and rivers. Rarely found away from wooded areas, where it nests in natural cavities or nest boxes. The male Hooded Merganser can voluntarily raise and lower its crest to show off the large white patch on its head. The female will "dump" eggs into other female Hooded Merganser nests, resulting in 20 to 25 eggs in some nests. Mergansers have been known to share a nesting cavity with Wood Ducks sitting side by side.

male

female

PILEATED WOODPECKER
Dryocopus pileatus

YEAR-ROUND

Size: 19" (48 cm)

Male: Crow-sized woodpecker with a black back and bright red crest. Long gray bill with red mustache. White leading edge of the wings flashes brightly when flying.

Female: same as male, but has a black forehead and lacks red mustache

Juvenile: similar to adult, only duller and browner overall

Nest: cavity; male and female excavate; 1 brood per year

Eggs: 3-5; white, unmarked

Incubation: 15-18 days; female and male incubate, the female during day, male at night

Fledging: 26-28 days; female and male feed young

Migration: non-migrator

Food: insects, will come to suet feeders

Compare: Red-headed Woodpecker (pg. 31) is about half the size, and has an all-red head, black back and white rump.

Stan's Notes: Our largest woodpecker, it excavates long oval holes up to several feet long in tree trunks, searching for insects. Large chips of wood lie at the base of excavated trees. Will drum on hollow branches, chimneys, etc., to announce its territory. Relatively shy bird that prefers large tracts of woodland. The young are fed regurgitated insects. Favorite food is carpenter ants.

soaring

OSPREY
Pandion haliaetus

Size: 24" (60 cm); up to 6-foot wingspan

Male: Large eagle-like bird with white chest, belly and black brown back. White head with a black streak across eyes. Large wings with black "wrist" marks.

Female: same as male, but with a necklace of brown streaking

Juvenile: same as adult

Nest: platform; female and male build; 1 brood per year

Eggs: 2-4; white with brown markings

Incubation: 32-42 days; female and male incubate

Fledging: 48-58 days; male and female feed young

Migration: complete, to Mexico, Central America and South America

Food: fish

Compare: Bald Eagle (pg. 43) is on average 10 inches larger, and has an all-white head and tail. The juvenile Bald Eagle is brown with white speckles. Look for a white belly and dark stripe across eye to identify Osprey.

Stan's Notes: Ospreys are in a family all their own. It is the only raptor that will plunge into the water to catch fish. Can hover for a few seconds before diving. Carries fish in a head-first position during flight for better aerodynamics. In flight, wings are angled (cocked) backward. Nests on man-made towers and tall dead trees. Recent studies show that male and female might mate for life, but don't migrate to the same wintering grounds.

soaring

juvenile

BALD EAGLE
Haliaeetus leucocephalus

YEAR-ROUND
WINTER

Size: 31-37" (79-94 cm); up to 7-foot wingspan

Male: Pure white head and tail contrast with dark brown-to-black body and wings. A large, curved yellow bill and yellow feet.

Female: same as male, only slightly larger

Juvenile: dark brown with white spots or speckles throughout body and wings, gray bill

Nest: massive platform; female and male build; 1 brood per year

Eggs: 2; off-white, unmarked

Incubation: 34-36 days; female and male incubate

Fledging: 75-90 days; female and male feed young

Migration: partial migrator, to southeastern states

Food: fish, carrion, ducks

Compare: Larger than Turkey Vulture (pg. 17), which lacks adult Bald Eagle's white head and tail. Turkey Vulture has two-toned wings and flies with its wings in a V shape, unlike the straight-out wing position of the Eagle.

Stan's Notes: Often seen soaring, this bird is making a comeback in Kentucky. Returns to the same nest every year, adding sticks, enlarging it to massive proportions, at times up to 1,000 pounds. In the midair mating ritual, one bird flips upside down, locking talons with another. Both tumble until they break apart to continue flying. Thought to mate for life, but will switch mates if not successful reproducing. Juveniles attain white head and tail at about 4 to 5 years of age.

BLUE-GRAY GNATCATCHER
Polioptila caerulea

SUMMER

Size: 4" (10 cm)

Male: Light blue head, back and wings, and white chest. Long black tail with white undertail, often held cocked above rest of the body. Black eyebrows. Prominent white eye ring.

Female: same as male, only grayer

Juvenile: same as adult

Nest: cup; female and male build; 1 brood a year

Eggs: 4-5; pale blue with dark markings

Incubation: 10-13 days; female and male incubate

Fledging: 10-12 days; female and male feed young

Migration: complete, to southern states, Bahamas and Central America

Food: insects

Compare: The only small blue bird with a black tail. Constantly flicks its tail up and down and from side to side. Very active near the nest, look for it flitting around upper branches in search of insects.

Stan's Notes: Found throughout Kentucky in a wide variety of forest types, listen for its wheezy call notes to help locate. A fun and easy bird to watch as it cocks and fans tail while calling. Returns to Kentucky by mid-April. In many years, it nests so early that by mid-June it is no longer defending territory, with most leaving the state by the end of August. Like many open woodland nesters, it is a common cowbird host. Although the population is abundant and widespread, it has been decreasing in the recent past.

TREE SWALLOW
Tachycineta bicolor

MIGRATION
SUMMER

Size: 5-6" (13-15 cm)

Male: Blue green in the spring and greener in fall. Appears to change color in direct sunlight. A white belly, a notched tail and pointed wing tips.

Female: similar to male, only duller

Juvenile: gray brown with a white belly and grayish breast band

Nest: cavity; female and male line former woodpecker cavity or nest box; 1 brood per year

Eggs: 4-6; white, unmarked

Incubation: 13-16 days; female incubates

Fledging: 20-24 days; female and male feed young

Migration: complete, to Mexico and Central America

Food: insects

Compare: Similar color to Purple Martin (pg. 57), but smaller and has white chest and belly. Barn Swallow (pg. 53) has rust belly and deeply forked tail.

Stan's Notes: The first swallow species to return each spring. Most common along ponds, lakes and agricultural fields. Is attracted to your yard with a nest box. Competes with the Eastern Bluebird for nest boxes. Will travel great distances to find dropped feathers to line its grass nest. Sometimes seen playing, chasing after dropped feathers. Often seen flying back and forth across fields, feeding on insects. Gathers in large flocks to migrate.

female pg. 83

male

INDIGO BUNTING
Passerina cyanea

SUMMER

Size: 5½" (14 cm)

Male: Vibrant blue finch-like bird. Scattered dark markings on wings and tail.

Female: light brown bird with faint markings

Juvenile: similar to female

Nest: cup; female builds; 2 broods per year

Eggs: 3-4; pale blue, unmarked

Incubation: 12-13 days; female incubates

Fledging: 10-11 days; female feeds young

Migration: complete, to southern states, Mexico and Central America

Food: insects, seeds, fruit, will visit seed feeders

Compare: Smaller than male Eastern Bluebird (pg. 55) and male Blue Grosbeak (pg. 51). Lacks the Bluebird's rusty red breast, and Grosbeak's chestnut-colored wing bars and large bill.

Stan's Notes: Usually only the males are noticed. Actually a black bird, as it doesn't have any blue pigment in its feathers. As with Blue Jays, the sunlight is refracted within the structure of the bunting's feathers, making them appear blue. Appears iridescent in direct sunlight. Molts to acquire body feathers with gray tips, which quickly wear off to reveal bright blue plumage. Males often sing from treetops to attract mates. Will come to feeders in spring before insects are plentiful. Mostly seen along woodland edges, feeding on insects. Migrates at night in flocks of five to ten birds. A late migrant, with males returning before the females and juveniles. Males nearly always return to previous year's nest site. Juveniles move to within a mile from birth site.

female pg. 95

male

BLUE GROSBEAK
Passerina caerulea

MIGRATION
SUMMER

Size: 7" (18 cm)

Male: An overall blue bird. Two chestnut-colored wing bars. A large gray-to-silver bill, black around base of bill.

Female: overall brown with darker wings and tail, two tan wing bars, large gray-to-silver bill

Juvenile: similar to female

Nest: cup; female builds; 1-2 broods per year

Eggs: 3-6; pale blue without markings

Incubation: 11-12 days; female incubates

Fledging: 9-10 days; female and male feed young

Migration: complete, to Central America, the Bahamas and Cuba

Food: insects, seeds, will come to seed feeders

Compare: Very similar to, but larger than, the more common male Indigo Bunting (pg. 49). Look for two chestnut wing bars and large heavy bill to distinguish from the Bunting.

Stan's Notes: Increasing population in Kentucky over the past 30 to 40 years, Blue Grosbeaks return to the state by mid-May. A bird of semi-open habitats such as overgrown fields, riversides, woodland edges. Will come to seed feeders, where it is often confused with the Indigo Bunting. Often seen twitching and spreading its tail. The first-year males show only some blue, obtaining the full complement of blue feathers in the second winter.

BARN SWALLOW
Hirundo rustica

SUMMER

Size: 7" (18 cm)

Male: A sleek swallow with a blue black back, a cinnamon belly and a reddish brown chin. White spots on long forked tail.

Female: same as male, only slightly duller

Juvenile: similar to adult, with tan belly and chin and shorter tail

Nest: cup; female and male build; 2 broods a year

Eggs: 4-5; white with brown markings

Incubation: 13-17 days; female incubates

Fledging: 18-23 days; female and male feed young

Migration: complete, to South America

Food: insects, prefers beetles, wasps and flies

Compare: Tree Swallow (pg. 47) has white belly and chin, and notched tail. The Chimney Swift (pg. 67) has narrow pointed tail with wings longer than the body. The Purple Martin (pg. 57) is nearly 2 inches larger and has a dark purple belly.

Stan's Notes: Of the six swallow species in Kentucky, this is the only one with a deeply forked tail. Unlike other swallows, the Barn Swallow rarely glides in flight, so look for continuous flapping. It builds a mud nest using up to 1,000 beak-loads of mud, often in or on barns. Nests in colonies of four to six, but nesting alone is not uncommon. Drinks while flying by skimming water or getting water from wet leaves. It also bathes while flying through the rain or sprinklers.

male

female

EASTERN BLUEBIRD
Sialia sialis

YEAR-ROUND

Size:	7" (18 cm)
Male:	Reminiscent of its larger cousin, American Robin, with a rusty red breast and white belly. Sky blue head, back and tail.
Female:	shares rusty red breast and white belly, but is grayer with faint blue tail and wings
Juvenile:	similar to female, with spots on chest, blue wing markings
Nest:	cavity, old woodpecker cavity or man-made nest box; female builds; 2 broods per year
Eggs:	4-5; pale blue, unmarked
Incubation:	12-14 days; female incubates
Fledging:	15-18 days; male and female feed young
Migration:	complete, to southern states
Food:	insects, fruit
Compare:	Male Indigo Bunting (pg. 49) is nearly all blue, lacking rusty red chest. The Blue Jay (pg. 59) is considerably larger with a crest and white markings.

Stan's Notes: A year-round resident in Kentucky, Eastern Bluebird populations sometimes drop due to unseasonably cold winters or cold, wet weather in spring. Although a permanent resident, some Eastern Bluebirds migrate each spring and autumn. Gathers in large family groups for migration and during winter. Bluebirds like open fields, pastures, roadsides and other open habitats. Will perch in trees or on fence posts and wait for grasshoppers and other insects. Gives a distinctive "chur-lee chur chur-lee" song. Young of first brood will help raise young of second.

male

female

PURPLE MARTIN
Progne subis

SUMMER

Size: 8½" (22 cm)

Male: A large swallow-shaped bird with a purple head, back and belly. Black wings and tail. Notched tail.

Female: gray purple head and back with a whitish belly, darker wings and tail

Juvenile: same as female

Nest: cavity; female and male line the cavity of house; 1 brood per year

Eggs: 4-5; white, unmarked

Incubation: 15-18 days; female incubates

Fledging: 26-30 days; male and female feed young

Migration: complete, to South America

Food: insects

Compare: The male is the only dark-purple-bellied swallow. Usually only seen in groups.

Stan's Notes: Largest swallow species in North America. Formerly nested in tree cavities, but now nearly exclusively nests in man-made nest boxes in Kentucky. Main diet consists of dragonflies, not mosquitoes as once thought. Often drinks and bathes while flying by skimming water or flying through rain. Returns to the same nest site each year. Males arrive before the females and yearlings. Often nests within 100 feet of a human dwelling and, in fact, the most successful colonies are located within this distance. Young strike out to form new colonies. Huge colonies gather in fall to migrate to South America.

BLUE JAY
Cyanocitta cristata

YEAR-ROUND

Size: 12" (30 cm)

Male: Large bright-light-blue and white bird with black necklace. Crest moves up and down at will. White face with a gray belly. White wing bars on blue wings. Black spots and a white tip on blue tail.

Female: same as male

Juvenile: same as adult, only duller

Nest: cup; the female and male build; 1-2 broods per year

Eggs: 4-5; green to blue with brown markings

Incubation: 16-18 days; female incubates

Fledging: 17-21 days; female and male feed young

Migration: non-migrator to partial migrator, will move around to find abundant food source

Food: insects, fruit, carrion, seeds, nuts, attracted to seed feeders

Compare: Eastern Bluebird (pg. 55) is much smaller and lacks the crest. The Belted Kingfisher (pg. 61) lacks vivid blue color and black necklace of the Blue Jay.

Stan's Notes: Highly intelligent bird, solving problems, gathering food and communicating more than other birds. Will scream like a hawk to scatter birds at a feeder before approaching. Known as the alarm of the forest, screaming at any intruders in the woods. Is known to eat eggs or young birds from nests of other birds. One of the few birds to cache food. Feathers don't have blue pigment; refracted sunlight casts blue light.

male

female

BELTED KINGFISHER
Ceryle alcyon

YEAR-ROUND

Size: 13" (33 cm)

Male: Large blue bird with white belly. Broad blue gray breast band and a ragged crest that is raised and lowered at will. Large head with a long, thick black bill. A small white spot directly in front of red brown eyes. Black wing tips with splashes of white that flash when flying.

Female: same as male, but with rusty breast band in addition to blue gray band, and rusty flanks

Juvenile: same as adult

Nest: cavity; female and male excavate; 1 brood per year

Eggs: 6-7; white, unmarked

Incubation: 23-24 days; female and male incubate

Fledging: 23-24 days; female and male feed young

Migration: complete, to southern states, Central and South America

Food: small fish

Compare: Similar in size to the Blue Jay (pg. 59), but Kingfisher is darker blue with larger, more ragged crest.

Stan's Notes: Seen perched on branches near the water, it dives headfirst for small fish and returns to a branch to eat. Has a loud machine-gun-like call. Excavates a deep cavity in bank of river or lake. Parents drop dead fish into water, teaching young to dive. Regurgitates pellets of bone after meals, being unable to pass bones through digestive tract. Mates recognize each other by call.

CHESTNUT-SIDED WARBLER
Dendroica pensylvanica

MIGRATION
SUMMER

Size: 5" (13 cm)

Male: A colorful combination of a yellow cap and black mask set against a white face, chin, chest and belly. Two yellow wing bars on gray wings. Chestnut-colored flanks.

Female: similar to male, but flanks duller brown

Juvenile: similar to female, a lime green head and back, a white eye ring, bright yellow wing bars, lacks chestnut sides

Nest: cup; female builds; 1 brood per year

Eggs: 3-5; white with brown markings

Incubation: 12-13 days; female incubates

Fledging: 10-12 days; female and male feed young

Migration: complete, to Central America

Food: insects, berries

Compare: Shares yellow cap with the Yellow-rumped Warbler (pg. 175), but lacks yellow sides and rump. The Yellow Warbler (pg. 253) is nearly all yellow and lacks the Chestnut's white chest and chestnut-colored flanks.

Stan's Notes: Prefers an open, young aspen forest. Look for this attractive warbler in spring, hopping high in the branches while it hunts for insects. You will usually only get a glimpse of this fast-moving warbler. Will hold its tail in an uplifted position, showing a white tail. Not uncommon for this bird to approach humans in defense of a nest site.

BROWN CREEPER
Certhia americana

Size: 5" (13 cm)

Male: A small, thin, nearly camouflaged bird with white belly, long stiff tail and thin curved bill. Obvious white line above dark eyes.

Female: same as male

Juvenile: same as adult

Nest: cup; female builds; unknown how many broods per year

Eggs: 5-6; white with tiny brown markings

Incubation: 14-17 days; female incubates, male feeds female during incubation

Fledging: 13-16 days; female and male feed young

Migration: partial migrator

Food: insects, nuts, seeds

Compare: Creeps up tree trunks, not down, like the White-breasted Nuthatch (pg. 173). Watch for Creeper to fly from the top of one trunk to the bottom of another, working its way to the top, looking for insects. Slightly larger than the Red-breasted Nuthatch (pg. 169), with a similar white stripe above eyes, but Creeper has a white belly, long tail and no black crown.

Stan's Notes: Utilizes camouflage coloring to defend itself by spreading out flat on a branch or tree trunk without moving. The young are able to follow the parents, creeping soon after fledging. Commonly seen in wooded areas. Often builds nest behind loose bark of dead or dying trees.

CHIMNEY SWIFT
Chaetura pelagica

SUMMER

Size: 5" (13 cm)

Male: Nondescript, swallow-shaped bird, usually only seen flying. Long, thin all-brown body with a pointed tail and head. Long swept-back wings are longer than body.

Female: same as male

Juvenile: same as adult

Nest: half cup; female and male build; 1 brood per year

Eggs: 4-5; white, unmarked

Incubation: 19-21 days; female and male incubate

Fledging: 28-30 days; female and male feed young

Migration: complete, to South America

Food: insects, while in flight

Compare: Considerably smaller than Purple Martin (pg. 57) and lacks Martin's iridescent purple color. Barn Swallow (pg. 53) has forked tail, compared with the pointed tail of the Chimney Swift. Tree Swallow (pg. 47) has white belly and blue green back.

Stan's Notes: One of the fastest flyers in the bird world. Spends all day flying, rarely perching. Bathes and drinks by skimming across water surfaces. Unique in-flight twittering call is often heard before bird is seen. Flies in groups, feeding on flying insects nearly 100 feet in the air. Often called the Flying Cigar due to its pointed body shape. Hundreds will nest and roost in large chimneys, hence the common name. Nest, made of tiny twigs, is cemented with saliva and attached to inside of chimney or hollow tree.

CHIPPING SPARROW
Spizella passerina

SUMMER

Size: 5" (13 cm)

Male: Small gray brown sparrow with a clear gray chest, rusty crown, white eyebrows with a black eye line, thin gray black bill and two faint wing bars.

Female: same as male

Juvenile: similar to adult, but has streaked chest and lacks rusty cap

Nest: cup; female builds; 2 broods per year

Eggs: 3-5; blue green with brown markings

Incubation: 11-14 days; female incubates

Fledging: 10-12 days; female and male feed young

Migration: complete, to southern states, Mexico and Central America

Food: insects, seeds, will come to ground feeders

Compare: Two inches smaller than the rusty-colored Fox Sparrow (pg. 93). Look for the clear gray chest of Chipping Sparrow.

Stan's Notes: A common garden or yard bird, often seen feeding on dropped seeds below feeders. Gathers in large family groups to feed each autumn in preparation for migration. Migrates at night in flocks of 20 to 30 birds. Received its common name from the male's fast "chip" call. Often just called Chippy. Nest is placed low in dense shrubs and is almost always lined with animal hair.

male pg. 227

female

HOUSE FINCH
Carpodacus mexicanus

YEAR-ROUND

Size: 5" (13 cm)

Female: A plain brown bird with a heavily streaked white chest.

Male: orange red face, chest and rump, a brown cap, brown marking behind eyes, brown wings streaked with white, white belly with brown streaks

Juvenile: similar to female

Nest: cup, sometimes in cavities; female builds; 2 broods per year

Eggs: 4-5; pale blue, lightly marked

Incubation: 12-14 days; female incubates

Fledging: 15-19 days; female and male feed young

Migration: non-migrator to partial migrator, will move around to find food

Food: seeds, fruit, leaf buds, will visit seed feeders

Compare: The female Purple Finch (pg. 85) is very similar, but has bold white eyebrows. The female American Goldfinch (pg. 245) has a clear chest and white wing bars. Similar to Pine Siskin (pg. 75), but lacks yellow wing bars and has a much larger bill than Siskin.

Stan's Notes: A relatively new bird to Kentucky (first reported in the early 1970s and first nests reported by 1981), it was originally introduced to Long Island, New York, in the 1940s from western America. A very social bird, it visits feeders in small flocks. Seems to prefer nesting in hanging flower baskets. Incubating female is fed by male. Loud and cheerful warbling song.

HOUSE WREN
Troglodytes aedon

Size: 5" (13 cm)

Male: A small all-brown bird with lighter brown marking on tail and wings. Brown, slightly curved bill. Often holds its tail erect.

Female: same as male

Juvenile: same as adult

Nest: cavity; female and male line just about any cavity; 2 broods per year

Eggs: 4-6; tan with brown markings

Incubation: 10-13 days; female and male incubate

Fledging: 12-15 days; female and male feed young

Migration: complete, to southern states and Mexico

Food: insects

Compare: Distinguished from Carolina Wren (pg. 79) by the lack of eye stripe.

Stan's Notes: A prolific songster, it will sing from dawn until dusk during the mating season. Easily attracted to nest boxes. In spring, the male chooses several prospective nesting cavities and places a few small twigs in each. Female inspects each, chooses one, and finishes the nest building. She will completely fill the nest cavity with uniformly small twigs, then line a small depression at back of cavity with pine needles and grass. Often has trouble fitting long twigs through nest cavity hole. Tries many different directions and approaches until successful.

PINE SISKIN
Carduelis pinus

WINTER

Size: 5" (13 cm)

Male: A small brown finch with heavily streaked back, breast and belly. Yellow wing bars and yellow at base of tail. Thin bill.

Female: similar to male, with less yellow

Juvenile: similar to adult, with a light yellow tinge throughout chest and chin

Nest: modified cup; the female builds; 2 broods per year

Eggs: 3-4; greenish blue with brown markings

Incubation: 12-13 days; female incubates

Fledging: 14-15 days; female and male feed young

Migration: irruptive, moves around the state in search of food

Food: seeds, insects, will come to seed feeders

Compare: Female American Goldfinch (pg. 245) lacks streaks and has white wing bars. Female House Finch (pg. 71) has streaked chest, but lacks yellow wing bars. Female Purple Finch (pg. 85) has bold white eyebrows.

Stan's Notes: Usually considered a winter finch, this bird can be seen in flocks of up to 20 individuals and is often seen with other finch species. More common in the northern half of Kentucky, but can be found throughout the state in heavy invasion years; it is absent from Kentucky in some winters. Comes to thistle feeders. Travels and breeds in small groups, with nests often only a few feet apart. Male feeds female during incubation. Juveniles lose yellow tint on chest and chin by late summer of first year.

SONG SPARROW
Melospiza melodia

Size: 5-6" (13-15 cm)

Male: Common brown sparrow with heavy dark streaks on chest coalescing into a central dark spot.

Female: same as male

Juvenile: similar to adult, finely streaked chest without central spot

Nest: cup; female builds; 2 broods per year

Eggs: 3-4; pale blue to green with reddish brown markings

Incubation: 12-14 days; female incubates

Fledging: 9-12 days; female and male feed young

Migration: complete, to southern states

Food: insects, seeds, rarely visits seed feeders

Compare: Similar to other brown sparrows, look for a heavily streaked chest with central dark spot.

Stan's Notes: Many Song Sparrow subspecies or varieties, but dark central spot carries through each variant. While the female builds another nest for second brood, the male often takes over feeding the young. Returns to similar area each year, defending a small territory by singing from thick shrubs. Common host of the Brown-headed Cowbird. Ground feeders, look for them to scratch simultaneously with both feet to expose seeds. Unlike many sparrow species, Song Sparrows rarely flock together.

CAROLINA WREN
Thryothorus ludovicianus

Size: 5½" (14 cm)

Male: Warm rusty-brown head and back with an orange yellow chest and belly. White throat and a prominent white eye stripe. A short stubby tail, often cocked up.

Female: same as male

Juvenile: same as adult

Nest: cavity; female and male build; 2 broods per year, sometimes 3

Eggs: 4-6; white, sometimes pink or creamy, with brown markings

Incubation: 12-14 days; female incubates

Fledging: 12-14 days; female and male feed young

Migration: non-migrator

Food: insects, fruit, few seeds

Compare: Similar to the House Wren (pg. 73), but the Carolina Wren is a lighter brown and has a prominent white eye stripe.

Stan's Notes: Mates are long-term, remaining together throughout the year in permanent territories. Will sing throughout the year. The male is known to sing up to 40 different song types, singing one song repeatedly before switching to another. Females also sing, resulting in duets. Male often takes over feeding the first brood of young while the female renests. Range expands northward in years with mild winters. Will nest in birdhouses or in the most unusual places, such as mailboxes, bumpers of cars, broken taillights or just about any other cavity. Found in woodland or brushy yards.

male pg. 179

female

DARK-EYED JUNCO
Junco hyemalis

Size: 5½" (14 cm)

Female: A round, dark-eyed bird with tan-to-brown chest, head and back. White belly. Ivory-to-pink bill. Since the outermost tail feathers are white, tail appears as a white V in flight.

Male: same as female, only slate gray to charcoal

Juvenile: similar to female, but has a streaked chest and head

Nest: cup; female and male build; 2 broods a year

Eggs: 3-5; white with reddish brown markings

Incubation: 12-13 days; female incubates

Fledging: 10-13 days; male and female feed young

Migration: complete, all across the U.S.

Food: seeds, insects, will come to seed feeders

Compare: Rarely confused with any other bird. Large flocks come to feed under bird feeders.

Stan's Notes: A common winter bird of Kentucky. Usually seen on the ground in small flocks. Migrates from Canada to Kentucky and beyond. Females tend to migrate farther south than males. Look for white outer tail feathers that flash in flight. Several junco species have now been combined into one, simply called Dark-eyed Junco. Most comfortable on the ground, juncos will "double-scratch" with both feet to expose seeds and insects. Consumes many weed seeds. A flocking bird, it adheres to a rigid social hierarchy with dominant birds chasing less dominant birds.

female

male pg. 49

INDIGO BUNTING
Passerina cyanea

SUMMER

Size: 5½" (14 cm)

Female: Light brown finch-like bird. Faint streaking on a light tan chest. Wings have a very faint blue cast with indistinct wing bars.

Male: vibrant blue finch-like bird, scattered dark markings on wings and tail

Juvenile: similar to female

Nest: cup; female builds; 2 broods per year

Eggs: 3-4; pale blue, unmarked

Incubation: 12-13 days; female incubates

Fledging: 10-11 days; female feeds young

Migration: complete, to southern states, Mexico and Central America

Food: insects, seeds, fruit, will visit seed feeders

Compare: Smaller than female Blue Grosbeak (pg. 95) and lacking the Grosbeak's tan wing bars. Similar to female finches. Female American Goldfinch (pg. 245) has white wing bars. Female Purple Finch (pg. 85) has white eye stripe and a heavily streaked chest. Female House Finch (pg. 71) also has a heavily streaked chest.

Stan's Notes: A secretive bird, usually only the males are seen. Males often sing from treetops to attract mates. Will come to feeders in spring before insects are plentiful. Mostly seen along woodland edges, feeding on insects. Migrates at night in flocks of five to ten birds. A late migrant, with males returning before the females and juveniles. Juveniles move to within a mile from birth site.

male pg. 229

female

PURPLE FINCH
Carpodacus purpureus

WINTER

Size: 6" (15 cm)

Female: A plain brown bird with a heavily streaked chest. Prominent white eyebrows.

Male: raspberry-red head, cap, breast, back and rump, brownish wings and tail

Juvenile: same as female

Nest: cup; female and male build; 1 brood a year

Eggs: 4-5; greenish blue with brown markings

Incubation: 12-13 days; female incubates

Fledging: 13-14 days; female and male feed young

Migration: irruptive, moves around the state in search of food

Food: seeds, insects, fruit, comes to seed feeders

Compare: The female House Finch (pg. 71) lacks the white eyebrows. The Pine Siskin (pg. 75) has yellow wing bars and a much smaller bill. Female American Goldfinch (pg. 245) has a clear chest and white wing bars.

Stan's Notes: Usually only seen during the winter, when flocks of Purple Finches leave their northern homes and move around in search of food. Travels in flocks of up to 50. Comes to seed feeders along with House Finches, making it hard to tell them apart. A rich loud song and a distinctive "tic" note is made only in flight. Not a purple color, the Latin name *purpureus* means "crimson" or other reddish color.

male

female

HOUSE SPARROW
Passer domesticus

YEAR-ROUND

Size: 6" (15 cm)

Male: Medium sparrow-like bird with large black spot on throat extending down to the chest. Brown back and single white wing bars. A gray belly and crown.

Female: all-light-brown bird, slightly smaller, lacks the black throat patch and single wing bars

Juvenile: similar to female

Nest: domed cup nest, within cavity; female and male build; 2-3 broods per year

Eggs: 4-6; white with brown markings

Incubation: 10-12 days; female incubates

Fledging: 14-17 days; female and male feed young

Migration: non-migrator, moves around to find food

Food: seeds, insects, fruit, comes to seed feeders

Compare: Lacks the rusty crown of Chipping Sparrow (pg. 69). Look for male House Sparrow's black bib. Female has a clear chest and no marking on head (cap).

Stan's Notes: Introduced from Europe to Central Park, New York, in 1850 and now found throughout North America. These birds are not really sparrows, but members of the Weaver Finch family, characterized by large, oversized domed nests. Constructs a nest containing scraps of plastic, paper and whatever else is available. Aggressive bird that will kill the young of other birds in order to take over a cavity. Familiar city bird, nearly always in flocks.

white-striped

tan-striped

WHITE-THROATED SPARROW
Zonotrichia albicollis

WINTER

Size: 6-7" (15-18 cm)

Male: A brown bird with gray tan chest and belly. Small yellow spot between the eyes (lore). Distinctive white or tan throat patch. White or tan stripes alternate with black stripes on crown. Color of the throat patch and crown stripes match.

Female: same as male

Juvenile: similar to adult, gray throat and eyebrows with heavily streaked chest

Nest: cup; female builds; 1 brood per year

Eggs: 4-6; varies between greenish, bluish and creamy white, with red brown markings

Incubation: 11-14 days; female incubates

Fledging: 10-12 days; female and male feed young

Migration: complete, to southern states and Mexico

Food: insects, seeds, fruit, visits ground feeders

Compare: The White-crowned Sparrow (pg. 91) lacks yellow lore and white or tan throat patch.

Stan's Notes: There are two color variations (polymorphic) of the White-throated Sparrow: white-striped or tan-striped. Studies have indicated the white-striped adults tend to mate with the tan-striped birds. No indication why. Nests are built on the ground under small trees in bogs and coniferous forests.

juvenile

WHITE-CROWNED SPARROW
Zonotrichia leucophrys

WINTER

Size: 6½-7½" (16-19 cm)

Male: A brown sparrow with a gray chest and a black-and-white striped crown. Small, thin pink bill.

Female: same as male

Juvenile: similar to adult, with brown stripes on the head instead of white

Nest: cup; female builds; 2 broods per year

Eggs: 3-5; varies between greenish, bluish and whitish, with red brown markings

Incubation: 11-14 days; female incubates

Fledging: 8-12 days; male and female feed young

Migration: complete, to southern states and Mexico

Food: insects, seeds, berries, visits ground feeders

Compare: The White-throated Sparrow (pg. 89) has a white or tan throat patch, and yellow spot between eyes and bill, with a blackish bill.

Stan's Notes: Doesn't nest in Kentucky. Males take most of the responsibility of raising young while females start second broods. Only 9 to 12 days separate the broods. Feeds on the ground by scratching backward with both feet at the same time. Usually seen in groups of up to 20 during spring and fall migrations.

FOX SPARROW
Passerella iliaca

WINTER

Size: 7" (18 cm)

Male: A plump rusty-red sparrow with a heavily streaked, rust-colored breast and solid rust tail. Head and back are mottled with gray.

Female: same as male

Juvenile: same as adult

Nest: cup; female builds; 2 broods per year

Eggs: 2-4; pale green with reddish markings

Incubation: 12-14 days; female incubates

Fledging: 10-11 days; female and male feed young

Migration: complete, to southern states

Food: insects, seeds, comes to feeders

Compare: Similar coloration as the Brown Thrasher (pg. 123), but the Fox Sparrow is smaller, plumper and has a smaller bill. Rusty color differentiates it from all other sparrows.

Stan's Notes: One of the largest sparrows, it is often only seen under seed feeders during spring and fall migrations. Scratches like a chicken with both feet at the same time to find seeds and insects. Nests on the ground in brush and along forest edges in Canada. The name "Sparrow" comes from the Anglo-Saxon word *spearwa*, which means "flutterer," as applied to any small bird. "Fox" refers to the bird's rusty color.

male pg. 51

female

BLUE GROSBEAK
Passerina caerulea

MIGRATION
SUMMER

Size: 7" (18 cm)

Female: Overall brown with darker wings and tail. Two tan wing bars. Large gray-to-silver bill.

Male: blue bird with two chestnut-colored wing bars, a large gray-to-silver bill with black around base of bill

Juvenile: similar to female

Nest: cup; female builds; 1-2 broods per year

Eggs: 3-6; pale blue without markings

Incubation: 11-12 days; female incubates

Fledging: 9-10 days; female and male feed young

Migration: complete, to Central America, the Bahamas and Cuba

Food: insects, seeds, will come to seed feeders

Compare: Very similar to, but larger than, the more common female Indigo Bunting (pg. 83). The female Indigo Bunting lacks the wing bars and large bill.

Stan's Notes: Increasing population in Kentucky over the past 30 to 40 years, Blue Grosbeaks return to the state by mid-May. A bird of semi-open habitats such as overgrown fields, riversides, woodland edges. Will come to seed feeders, where it is often confused with the Indigo Bunting. Often seen twitching and spreading its tail. The first-year males show only some blue, obtaining the full complement of blue feathers in the second winter.

1 year old

Bohemian
Waxwing

CEDAR WAXWING
Bombycilla cedrorum

YEAR-ROUND

Size: 7½" (19 cm)

Male: Very sleek-looking gray-to-brown bird with pointed crest, light yellow belly and bandit-like black mask. Tip of tail is bright yellow and the tips of wings look as if they have been dipped in red wax.

Female: same as male

Juvenile: slightly smaller, overall gray, lacks red wing tips, black mask and sleek appearance, has a heavily streaked chest

Nest: cup; female and male build; 1 brood a year, occasionally 2

Eggs: 4-6; pale blue with brown markings

Incubation: 10-12 days; female incubates

Fledging: 14-18 days; female and male feed young

Migration: partial migrator

Food: cedar cones, fruit, insects

Compare: Similar to its larger, less common cousin, Bohemian Waxwing (see inset), which has white on wings and rust under tail.

Stan's Notes: The name is derived from its red wax-like wing tips and preference for eating small blueberry-like cones of the cedar. Mostly seen in flocks, moving from area to area, looking for berries. Wanders in winter to find available food supplies. Seen more often in winter because naked branches reveal its presence. In summer, before berries are abundant, it feeds on insects. Spends most of its time at the tops of tall trees. Listen for the very high-pitched "sreee" whistling sounds it constantly makes. Obtains mask after first year.

97

male pg. 5

female

BROWN-HEADED COWBIRD
Molothrus ater

SUMMER

Size:	7½" (19 cm)
Female:	Dull brown bird with no obvious markings. Pointed, sharp gray bill.
Male:	glossy black bird, chocolate brown head
Juvenile:	similar to female, only dull gray color and a streaked chest
Nest:	no nest; lays eggs in nests of other birds
Eggs:	5-7; white with brown markings
Incubation:	10-13 days; host bird incubates eggs
Fledging:	10-11 days; host birds feed young
Migration:	complete, to southern states
Food:	insects, seeds, will come to seed feeders
Compare:	In the blackbird family. The slightly larger female Red-winged Blackbird (pg. 113) has white eyebrows and a streaked chest. The European Starling (pg. 7) has speckles, a long, pointed yellow bill and short tail.

Stan's Notes: Of about 750 species of parasitic birds worldwide, this is the only parasitic bird in Kentucky, laying all eggs in host birds' nests, leaving others to raise its young. Cowbirds are known to have laid eggs in nests of over 200 species of birds. Some birds reject cowbird eggs, but most raise them, even to the exclusion of their own young. Look for warblers and other birds feeding young birds twice their own size. At one time cowbirds followed bison to feed on the insects attracted to the animals.

male pg. 3

female

EASTERN TOWHEE
Pipilo erythrophthalmus

YEAR-ROUND

Size: 7-8" (18-20 cm)

Female: A mostly light brown bird. Rusty red brown sides and white belly. Long brown tail with white tip. Short, stout, pointed bill and rich red eyes. White wing patches flash in flight.

Male: similar to female, but is black, not brown

Juvenile: light brown, a heavily streaked head, chest and belly, long dark tail with white tip

Nest: cup; female builds; 2 broods per year

Eggs: 3-4; creamy white with brown markings

Incubation: 12-13 days; female incubates

Fledging: 10-12 days; female and male feed young

Migration: complete, to southern states and South America

Food: insects, seeds, fruit, visits ground feeders

Compare: Slightly smaller than the American Robin (pg. 193). Female Rose-breasted Grosbeak (pg. 105) has a heavily streaked chest and white eyebrows.

Stan's Notes: Common name comes from its distinctive "tow-hee" call given by both sexes. Mostly known for its characteristic call that sounds like, "Drink-your-tea!" Seen hopping backward with both feet to rake up leaf litter (bilateral scratching), in search of insects and seeds. The female broods, but male does most of the feeding of young. White-eyed form in southern states, red-eyed elsewhere.

HORNED LARK
Eremophila alpestris

YEAR-ROUND
WINTER

Size: 7-8" (18-20 cm)

Male: A sleek tan-to-brown bird. Black necklace with yellow chin and black bill. Two tiny "horns" on top of the head, which can be difficult to see. Black tail with white outer feathers noticeable in flight.

Female: same as male, only duller, "horns" are less noticeable

Juvenile: lacks the black markings and yellow chin, doesn't form "horns" until second year

Nest: ground; female builds; 2 broods per year

Eggs: 3-4; gray with brown markings

Incubation: 11-12 days; female incubates

Fledging: 9-12 days; female and male feed young

Migration: non-migrator to partial in Kentucky

Food: seeds, insects

Compare: Larger than the House Sparrow (pg. 87). Look for a black mark on Horned Lark's face and neck.

Stan's Notes: The only true lark in North America. A year-round resident, but also moves around to find food (seasonal movement). Larks are birds of open ground. Common in rural areas, almost always seen in large flocks at country roads. Population increased over the past 100 years due to clearing land for farming. May have up to three broods per year because they get such an early start. Females perform a fluttering distraction display if nest is disturbed. Females can renest about seven days after brood fledges. The name "Lark" comes from the Middle English word *laverock*, or "a lark."

female

male pg. 25

ROSE-BREASTED GROSBEAK
Pheucticus ludovicianus

MIGRATION
SUMMER

Size: 7-8" (18-20 cm)

Female: Plump, heavily streaked brown and white bird with obvious white eyebrows. Orange yellow wing linings.

Male: black-and-white bird with large, triangular rose patch in center of chest, rosy-red wing linings, large ivory bill

Juvenile: same as female

Nest: cup; the female and male build; 1-2 broods per year

Eggs: 3-5; blue green with brown markings

Incubation: 13-14 days; female and male incubate

Fledging: 9-12 days; female and male feed young

Migration: complete, to Mexico, Central America and South America

Food: insects, seeds, fruit, comes to seed feeders

Compare: Female looks like a large sparrow. Female is larger and has a more distinctive eyebrow mark than female Purple Finch (pg. 85). The female House Finch (pg. 71) has no eyebrow mark.

Stan's Notes: Both female and male sing, but the male sings much louder and clearer. A rich, robin-like song. "Grosbeak" refers to its large bill, used to crush seeds. Male's red breast patch varies in size and shape in each individual. Males arrive first in spring, joined by females several days later. Late to arrive in spring and early to leave in autumn. Often prefers mature deciduous forest for nesting.

WOOD THRUSH
Hylocichla mustelina

Size: 8" (20 cm)

Male: Reddish brown head, back and wings with color fading into a brown tail. Distinctive white chest, belly and sides covered with black spots. White ring around black eyes, obvious on a black-streaked white face.

Female: same as male

Juvenile: similar to adult

Nest: cup; female builds; 1-2 broods per year

Eggs: 2-4; greenish blue without markings

Incubation: 13-14 days; female incubates

Fledging: 11-12 days; female and male feed young

Migration: complete, to Central and South America

Food: insects, fruit

Compare: Similar body shape as the American Robin (pg. 193), but lacks the Robin's red breast. Similar rusty color of the Brown Thrasher (pg. 123), but Thrasher has a much longer rusty red tail and bright yellow eyes, compared with the shorter brown tail and black eyes of Thrush.

Stan's Notes: Well known for its liquid flute-like calls, which are heard deep within woodlots throughout Kentucky. Returns to the state during the last two weeks of April after spending the winter in southern coastal states, and Central and South America. Returns to the same woodland year after year. Often seen on the ground, hopping around like a robin in search of insects.

winter

breeding

SPOTTED SANDPIPER
Actitis macularius

MIGRATION
SUMMER

Size: 8" (20 cm)

Male: Long dull yellow legs and a long bill. Olive brown back. A white chest and white line over the eyes. Breeding has black spots on chest. Lacks breast spots in fall and winter.

Female: same as male

Juvenile: similar to winter adult, with a darker bill

Nest: ground; female and male build; 2 broods per year

Eggs: 3-4; brownish with brown markings

Incubation: 20-24 days; male incubates

Fledging: 17-21 days; male feeds young

Migration: complete, to southern states and South America

Food: aquatic insects

Compare: Smaller than Lesser Yellowlegs (pg. 121). Look for Spotted Sandpiper to bob its tail up and down while standing. Look for the breeding Spotted Sandpiper's black spots extending from chest down to abdomen.

Stan's Notes: One of the more common sandpipers. Constantly bobs its tail while standing and walks as if delicately balanced. Flies with wings held in a cup-like arc, rarely lifting them above a horizontal plane. Is able to fly straight up out of water. One of the few shorebirds that actually dives underwater if pursued. Female mates with multiple males and lays eggs in up to five different nests. Male incubates and cares for young. In winter plumage, it lacks spots.

male pg. 235

female

YEAR-ROUND

Size: 8-9" (20-22.5 cm)

Female: Buff brown bird with tinges of red on crest and wings, a black mask and large red bill.

Male: red bird with a black mask extending from face down to chin and throat, large red bill and crest

Juvenile: same as female, with blackish gray bill

Nest: cup; female builds; 2-3 broods per year

Eggs: 3-4; bluish white with brown markings

Incubation: 12-13 days; female and male incubate

Fledging: 9-10 days; female and male feed young

Migration: non-migrator

Food: seeds, insects, fruit, comes to seed feeders

Compare: Female Cardinal appears similar to the juvenile Cardinal. Look for the female's bright red bill.

Stan's Notes: A familiar backyard bird. Look for the male feeding female during courtship. Male feeds young of the first brood by himself while female builds second nest. The name comes from the Latin word *cardinalis*, which means "important." Very territorial in spring, it will fight its own reflection in a window. Non-territorial during winter, gathering in small flocks of up to 20 birds. Both the male and female sing, and can be heard anytime of year. Listen for its "whata-cheer-cheer-cheer" territorial call in spring.

female

male
pg. 9

RED-WINGED BLACKBIRD
Agelaius phoeniceus

Size: 8½" (22 cm)

Female: Heavily streaked brown bird with a pointed brown bill and white eyebrows.

Male: jet black bird with red and yellow patches on upper wings, pointed black bill

Juvenile: same as female

Nest: cup; female builds; 2-3 broods per year

Eggs: 3-4; bluish green with brown markings

Incubation: 10-12 days; female incubates

Fledging: 11-14 days; female and male feed young

Migration: complete, to southern states, Mexico and Central America

Food: seeds, insects, will come to seed feeders

Compare: Slightly larger than female Brown-headed Cowbird (pg. 99), which lacks the white eyebrows and streaks on chest. Similar to female Rose-breasted Grosbeak (pg. 105), only a thinner body and pointed bill.

Stan's Notes: One of the most widespread and numerous birds in Kentucky. It is a sure sign of spring when Red-winged Blackbirds return to the marshes. Flocks of up to 100,000 birds have been reported. Males return before the females and defend territories by singing from the tops of surrounding vegetation. Will repeat call from top of cattail while showing off its red and yellow wing bars (epaulets). Nests are usually over shallow water in thick stands of cattails. They feed mostly on seeds in spring and fall, switching to insects during summer. Females choose mate.

113

in flight

COMMON NIGHTHAWK
Chordeiles minor

SUMMER

Size: 9" (22.5 cm)

Male: A camouflaged brown and white bird with white chin. A distinctive white band across wings and the tail, seen only in flight.

Female: similar to male, but with tan chin, lacks the white tail band

Juvenile: same as adult

Nest: no nest; lays eggs on the ground, usually on rocks, or on rooftop; 1 brood per year

Eggs: 2; cream with lavender markings

Incubation: 19-20 days; female and male incubate

Fledging: 20-21 days; female and male feed young

Migration: complete, to South America

Food: insects caught in air

Compare: Male Whip-poor-will (pg. 117) is similar in size, but much browner. Look for the white chin and wing band of Nighthawk, seen in flight. Much larger than the Chimney Swift (pg. 67). Look for the obvious white wing band of Common Nighthawk in flight.

Stan's Notes: Usually only seen flying at dusk or after sunset, but not uncommon during day. Very noisy bird, repeating a "peenting" call during flight. Alternates slow wing beats with bursts of quick wing beats. Prolific insect eater. Prefers gravel rooftops for nesting. Male's distinctive springtime mating ritual is a steep diving flight terminated with a loud popping noise. One of the first birds to migrate each fall. Can be more common in cities than in country.

WHIP-POOR-WILL
Caprimulgus vociferus

SUMMER

Size: 10" (25 cm)

Male: Mottled brown and black. Distinctive black chin and a white U-shaped throat marking.

Female: same as male, but has a brown chin and tan throat marking

Juvenile: similar to adult

Nest: no nest; female lays eggs on ground; 1-2 broods per year

Eggs: 2; white with brown markings

Incubation: 19-20 days; female and male incubate

Fledging: 18-20 days; female and male feed young

Migration: complete, to Mexico, Central America and South America

Food: insects

Compare: Male Common Nighthawk (pg. 115) has a distinctive white band across wings (seen in flight), which the Whip-poor-will lacks. Nighthawk is commonly seen flying, while Whip-poor-will is rarely seen flying.

Stan's Notes: A very well-known bird in Kentucky, although it is rarely seen. Its repetitive nocturnal "whip-poor-will" call, usually heard only in the spring, is loved by many and hated by others. Nothing can be done to stop the nocturnal calling despite how much sleep you are losing. Generally found in woodland, Whip-poor-wills sit parallel on a branch during the day. They don't build nests, but lay eggs on the ground, selecting sites along forest edges. The male will care for its young if the female starts a second brood.

male

female

YEAR-ROUND

Size: 10" (25 cm)

Male: Short, stocky, mostly brown bird with short gray tail. A prominent white eye stripe and white chin. Reddish brown sides and belly, often with black lines and dots.

Female: similar to male, but with a buff brown eye stripe and chin

Juvenile: smaller and duller than adult

Nest: ground; the female and male build; 1 brood per year

Eggs: 12-15; white to creamy, unmarked

Incubation: 23-24 days; female and male incubate

Fledging: 6-7 days; female and male feed young

Migration: non-migrator

Food: insects, seeds, fruit, will come to ground feeders offering corn and millet

Compare: Much smaller than Ruffed Grouse (pg. 145) and lacks squared tail. Look for the light eyebrows and chin of the Bobwhite.

Stan's Notes: Prefers shrubs, orchards, hedgerows and pastures. Moves around in small flocks of 20 birds (often family members), called a covey. The covey often rests together during the night, in a tight circle with tails together and heads facing outward, to watch for predators. Males and females perform distraction displays when nests or young are threatened. Nest is a depression in the ground lined with grass. Often pulls nearby vegetation over nest to help conceal it. Male gives a rising whistle, "bob-white," heard mainly in spring and summer. Also gives a single "hoy" call year-round.

LESSER YELLOWLEGS
Tringa flavipes

MIGRATION

Size: 10-11" (25-28 cm)

Male: Typical sandpiper-type bird with a brown back and wings, and lightly streaked white breast and belly. A thin, straight black bill and long yellow legs.

Female: same as male

Juvenile: same as adult

Nest: ground; female builds; 1 brood per year

Eggs: 3-4; yellowish with brown markings

Incubation: 22-23 days; male and female incubate

Fledging: 18-20 days; male and female lead young to food

Migration: complete, to South America

Food: aquatic insects, tiny fish

Compare: The breeding Spotted Sandpiper (pg. 109) is smaller. Look for the straight black bill and long yellow legs of Lesser Yellowlegs.

Stan's Notes: Usually seen in large flocks, it combs shorelines and mud flats looking for aquatic insects. Most often seen in the head down, tail up position, walking along, looking to snatch up food. Uses its long straight bill to pluck insects and tiny fish from water. Very shy bird that quite often moves into the water prior to taking flight. Has a variety of "flight" notes that it gives when taking off. A member of the group of sandpipers called Tattlers, all of which scream alarm calls when taking flight. Nests on marshes in spruce forests of central Alaska and central Canada. The nest is a simple depression atop a mound of earth.

BROWN THRASHER
Toxostoma rufum

Size: 11" (28 cm)

Male: A rusty red bird with long tail and heavily streaked chest and belly. Two white wing bars. Long curved bill. Bright yellow eyes.

Female: same as male

Juvenile: same as adult, eye color is grayish

Nest: cup; female and male build; 2 broods a year

Eggs: 4-5; pale blue with brown markings

Incubation: 11-14 days; female and male incubate

Fledging: 10-13 days; female and male feed young

Migration: complete, to southern states

Food: insects, fruit

Compare: Slightly larger in size and similar in shape to the American Robin (pg. 193) and Gray Catbird (pg. 189), but the Thrasher has a streaked chest and rusty color. Similar rusty color as Fox Sparrow (pg. 93), but Brown Thrasher is larger and thinner. The Wood Thrush (pg. 107) has a shorter brown tail and black eyes, compared with Thrasher's longer rusty red tail and yellow eyes.

Stan's Notes: A prodigious songster, often found in thick shrubs where it sings deliberate musical phrases, repeating each twice. The male has the largest documented song repertoire of all North American birds, with over 1,100 song types. Is often seen quickly flying or running in and out of thick or dense shrubs.

KILLDEER
Charadrius vociferus

SUMMER

Size: 11" (28 cm)

Male: An upland shorebird with two black bands around the neck like a necklace. A brown back and white belly. Bright reddish-orange rump, visible in flight.

Female: same as male

Juvenile: similar to adult, but only one neck band

Nest: ground; male builds; 2 broods per year

Eggs: 3-5; tan with brown markings

Incubation: 24-28 days; male and female incubate

Fledging: 25 days; male and female lead their young to food

Migration: complete, to southern states, Mexico and Central America

Food: insects

Compare: Only shorebird with two black neck bands.

Stan's Notes: This bird is known for its broken wing impression, which draws intruders away from nest. Once clear of the nest, the Killdeer takes flight. Nests are only a slight depression in a gravel area, often very difficult to see. Young look like miniature adults on stilts when first hatched. Able to follow parents and peck for insects soon after birth. Is technically classified as a shorebird, but doesn't live at the shore. Often found in vacant fields or along railroads. Has a very distinctive "kill-jer" call.

male

female

AMERICAN KESTREL
Falco sparverius

YEAR-ROUND

Size: 10-12" (25-30 cm)

Male: Rusty brown back and tail. A white chest with dark spots. Double black vertical lines on white face. Blue gray wings. Distinctive wide black band with a white edge on tip of rusty tail.

Female: similar to male, slightly larger, but has rusty brown wings and dark bands on tail

Juvenile: same as adult

Nest: cavity; doesn't build a nest within; 1 brood per year

Eggs: 4-5; white with brown markings

Incubation: 29-31 days; male and female incubate

Fledging: 30-31 days; female and male feed young

Migration: complete, to southern states and Central America, small percentage non-migrator

Food: insects, small mammals and birds, reptiles

Compare: Similar to other falcons. Look for the two vertical black stripes on face of Kestrel. No other small bird of prey has rusty-colored back or tail.

Stan's Notes: Formerly called Sparrow Hawk due to its small size. Could be called Grasshopper Hawk because it eats many grasshoppers. Hovers near roads before diving for prey. Adapts quickly to a wooden nest box. Has pointed swept-back wings, seen in flight. Perches nearly upright. Kestrels are rare raptors in that males and females have quite different markings. Watch for them to pump their tails up and down after landing on perches.

female

male

NORTHERN FLICKER
Colaptes auratus

YEAR-ROUND

Size: 12" (30 cm)

Male: Brown and black woodpecker with a large white rump patch visible only when flying. Black necklace above a speckled breast. Red spot on nape of neck and black mustache.

Female: same as male, lacking black mustache

Juvenile: same as adult

Nest: cavity; female and male excavate; 1 brood per year

Eggs: 5-8; white, unmarked

Incubation: 11-14 days; female and male incubate

Fledging: 25-28 days; female and male feed young

Migration: complete, to southern states

Food: insects, especially ants and beetles

Compare: Yellow-bellied Sapsucker (pg. 27) is smaller, and has red chin and forehead. Red-bellied Woodpecker (pg. 33) has a black-and-white zebra-striped back, red patch on head and lacks mustache. Flickers are the only brown-backed woodpeckers in Kentucky.

Stan's Notes: The flicker is the only woodpecker to regularly feed on the ground, preferring ants and beetles. Produces antacid saliva to neutralize the acidic defense of ants. Male usually selects a nest site, taking up to 12 days to excavate. Some have been successful attracting flickers to nest boxes stuffed with sawdust. In flight, it flashes golden yellow under wings and tail, and undulates deeply while giving a loud "wacka-wacka" call.

MOURNING DOVE
Zenaida macroura

YEAR-ROUND

Size: 12" (30 cm)

Male: Smooth fawn-colored dove with gray patch on the head. Iridescent pink, green around neck. Single black spot behind and below eyes. Black spots on wings and tail. Pointed wedge-shaped tail with white edges.

Female: similar to male, lacking iridescent pink and green neck feathers

Juvenile: spotted and streaked

Nest: platform; female and male build; 2 broods per year

Eggs: 2; white, unmarked

Incubation: 13-14 days; male and female incubate, the male during day, female at night

Fledging: 12-14 days; female and male feed young

Migration: partial migrator, will move around to find food, or complete, to southern states

Food: seeds, will come to seed feeders

Compare: Smaller than Rock Pigeon (pg. 199), lacks its wide range of color combinations.

Stan's Notes: Name comes from its mournful cooing. A ground feeder, its head bobs as it walks. One of the few birds able to drink without lifting head, same as Rock Pigeon. Parents feed young (squab) a regurgitated liquid called crop-milk the first few days of life. Flimsy platform nest of twigs often falls apart in a storm. Wind rushing through wing feathers in flight creates a characteristic whistling sound.

YELLOW-BILLED CUCKOO
Coccyzus americanus

SUMMER

Size: 12" (30 cm)

Male: Grayish brown head, back, wings and tail. Undertail distinctively patterned with bold black and white spots and lines. A white chin, chest and belly, and long downward-curved bill. Lower bill (mandible) is yellow.

Female: same as male

Juvenile: similar to adult, undertail lacks bold black and white pattern, bill lacks yellow

Nest: platform; the female and male build; 1-2 broods per year

Eggs: 2-6; light blue without markings

Incubation: 9-11 days; female and male incubate

Fledging: 7-9 days; female and male feed young

Migration: complete, to South America

Food: insects

Compare: The large-sized, curved bill and bold black and white undertail markings make this bird hard to confuse with others.

Stan's Notes: A common summer resident throughout Kentucky. Found in a wide variety of habitats, but usually nests along forest edges. Often will place a flimsy stick nest in a densely covered tree fork. Unlike many other birds, the young do not hatch at the same time (asynchronously). There can be many days between first and last to hatch. A very short egg-to-fledging time with some young leaving the nest (fledging) after only one week. The first to fledge are attended by the male, while the female cares for the rest in the nest. Is declining in population in many states.

PIED-BILLED GREBE
Podilymbus podiceps

Size: 13" (33 cm)

Male: Small brown water bird with a black chin and black ring around a thick, chicken-like ivory bill. White puffy patch under the tail. Has an unmarked brown bill during winter.

Female: same as male

Juvenile: paler than adult, with white spots and gray chest, belly and bill

Nest: floating platform; female and male build; 1 brood per year

Eggs: 5-7; bluish white, unmarked

Incubation: 22-24 days; female and male incubate

Fledging: 22-24 days; female and male feed young

Migration: complete, to southern states, Mexico and Central America

Food: crayfish, aquatic insects, fish

Compare: The smallest brown water bird that dives underwater for long periods of time.

Stan's Notes: A common water bird during migration. Often seen diving for crayfish, aquatic insects and fish. It slowly sinks like a submarine when disturbed. Formerly called Hell-diver because of the length of time it stays submerged. Can surface far away from where it went under. Builds a platform nest on a floating mat in the water. Particularly sensitive to pollution. Adapted well to life on the water, with short wings, lobed toes and legs set close to rear of body. While swimming is easy, it is very awkward on ground. The name "Grebe" probably came from the Old English word *krib*, meaning "crest," a reference to the Great Crested Grebe found in Europe.

135

male

female

BLUE-WINGED TEAL
Anas discors

MIGRATION

Size:	15-16" (38-40 cm)
Male:	Small, plain-looking brown duck speckled with black. A gray head with a large white crescent-shaped mark at base of bill. Black tail with small white patch. Blue wing patch (speculum) usually only seen in flight.
Female:	duller version of male, lacks facial crescent mark and white tail markings
Juvenile:	same as female
Nest:	ground; female builds; 1 brood per year
Eggs:	8-11; creamy white
Incubation:	23-27 days; female incubates
Fledging:	35-44 days; female feeds young
Migration:	complete, to southern states and Central America
Food:	aquatic plants, seeds, aquatic insects
Compare:	Nearly half the size of the female Mallard (pg. 161). The female Blue-winged Teal is similar to the female Wood Duck (pg. 149), but lacks the Wood Duck's bright white eye ring and crest.

Stan's Notes: Male leaves female near end of incubation. Female will perform distraction display to protect nest and young. Nest is built some distance from water. Planting crops and cultivating to pond edges are causing a decline in population.

male pg. 35

female

LESSER SCAUP
Aythya affinis

MIGRATION
WINTER

Size: 16-17" (40-43 cm)

Female: Overall brown duck with dull white patch at base of light-gray bill. Yellow eyes.

Male: white and gray, the chest and head appear nearly black but head appears purple with green highlights in direct sun, yellow eyes

Juvenile: same as female

Nest: ground; female builds; 1 brood per year

Eggs: 8-14; olive buff without markings

Incubation: 22-28 days; female incubates

Fledging: 45-50 days; female teaches young to feed

Migration: complete, southern states, northern South America, Central America

Food: aquatic plants and insects

Compare: Male Blue-winged Teal (pg. 137) is smaller and has bright white crescent-shaped patch near base of bill.

Stan's Notes: A common diving duck in Kentucky. Often seen in large flocks on area lakes, ponds and sewage lagoons. Usually only seen during spring and fall migrations. When observed in flight, note the bold white stripe under the wings. Interesting baby-sitting arrangement in which the young form groups tended by one to three adult females.

soaring

BROAD-WINGED HAWK
Buteo platypterus

MIGRATION
SUMMER

Size: 14-19" (36-48 cm)

Male: A hawk slightly smaller than the American Crow, the Broad-winged has a brown back and rusty red barring on chest. The tail has two or three wide black-and-white bands. White under wings with black "fingertips," as seen in flight.

Female: same as male

Juvenile: tail bands narrower and more numerous, a brown-streaked chest and belly

Nest: platform; female and male build, but the female finishes; 1 brood per year

Eggs: 2-3; off-white with brown markings

Incubation: 28-32 days; female incubates, male feeds female during incubation

Fledging: 34-35 days; female and male feed young

Migration: complete, to Central and South America

Food: small mammals, small birds, large insects, snakes, frogs

Compare: Similar in size to Cooper's Hawk (pg. 201), but with wider, shorter tail. Larger than Sharp-shinned Hawk (pg. 197). Look for the alternating black-and-white tail bands.

Stan's Notes: A very common hawk in eastern Kentucky. Often seen in large groups (kettles) migrating early in autumn. Spends most of its time hunting snakes, small birds and frogs in dense woodland. Short round wings propel it through dense woods. Will scream "call" repetitively when intruders are near the nest.

141

soaring

RED-SHOULDERED HAWK
Buteo lineatus

YEAR ROUND

Size: 15-19" (38-48 cm); up to 3½-foot wingspan

Male: Reddish (cinnamon) head, shoulders, chest and belly. Wings and back are dark brown with white spots. Long tail with thin white bands and wide black bands. Obvious red wing linings, seen in flight.

Female: same as male

Juvenile: similar to adult, lacking the red color, white chest with dark spots

Nest: platform; female and male build; 1 brood per year

Eggs: 2-4; white with dark markings

Incubation: 27-29 days; female and male incubate

Fledging: 39-45 days; female and male feed young

Migration: non-migrator to partial migrator, winters in the U.S.

Food: reptiles, amphibians, large insects, birds

Compare: Sharp-shinned Hawk (pg. 197) is smaller and lacks Red-shouldered's reddish head and belly. Larger than the Cooper's Hawk (pg. 201), which has a slimmer body and longer tail.

Stan's Notes: A common hawk of Kentucky forests, preferring to hunt along forest edges. Spots snakes, frogs and other prey while perched. Often seen flapping with an alternating gliding pattern. Mates when 2 to 3 years old. Stays in same territory for many years. Nest building starts in February, with young leaving nests by June.

RUFFED GROUSE
Bonasa umbellus

YEAR-ROUND

Size: 16-19" (40-48 cm)

Male: Brown chicken-like bird with long squared tail. Wide black band near tip of tail. Is able to fan tail like a turkey. Tuft of feathers on the head stands like a crown. Black ruffs on sides of neck.

Female: same as male, but less obvious neck ruffs

Juvenile: same as female

Nest: ground; female builds; 1 brood per year

Eggs: 9-12; tan with light brown markings

Incubation: 23-24 days; female incubates

Fledging: 10-12 days; female leads young to food

Migration: non-migrator

Food: seeds, insects, fruit, leaf buds

Compare: Much larger than the Northern Bobwhite (pg. 119) and lacks Bobwhite's eye stripe. Look for feathered tuft on head and black neck ruffs.

Stan's Notes: A common bird of deep woods. Often seen in aspen or other trees, feeding on leaf buds. Grows bristles on its feet during winter to serve as snowshoes. If there is enough snow, it will dive into a snowbank to roost at night. In spring, male raises crest (tuft), fans tail feathers, and stands on logs and drums with wings to attract females. Drumming sound comes from cupped wings moving air, not pounding on chest or log. Females perform distraction display to protect young. Two color types, red and gray, most apparent in the tail. Black ruffs around the neck gave rise to its common name.

male pg. 37

female

HOODED MERGANSER
Lophodytes cucullatus

YEAR-ROUND
MIGRATION

Size: 16-19" (40-48 cm)

Female: Sleek brown and rust bird with a red head. Ragged "hair" on back of head. Long, thin brown bill.

Male: same size and shape as female, but black back and rust sides, crest "hood" raises to reveal large white patch, long black bill

Juvenile: similar to female

Nest: cavity; female lines old woodpecker hole; 1 brood per year

Eggs: 10-12; white, unmarked

Incubation: 32-33 days; female incubates

Fledging: 71 days; female feeds young

Migration: complete, to Gulf coast and Mexico

Food: small fish, aquatic insects

Compare: Larger than female Lesser Scaup (pg. 139), which has a dull white patch at base of bill. Look for the long thin bill and ragged "hair" feathers on the back of head to identify the female Merganser.

Stan's Notes: A small diving bird of shallow-water ponds, sloughs, lakes and rivers. Rarely found away from wooded areas, where it nests in natural cavities or nest boxes. The female will "dump" eggs into other female Hooded Merganser nests, resulting in 20 to 25 eggs in some nests. The male Hooded Merganser can voluntarily raise and lower its crest to show off the large white patch on its head. Mergansers have been known to share a nesting cavity with Wood Ducks sitting side by side.

147

male pg. 213

female

WOOD DUCK
Aix sponsa

SUMMER
WINTER

Size: 17-20" (43-50 cm)

Female: A small brown dabbling duck. Bright white eye ring and a not-so-obvious crest. A blue patch on wing is often hidden.

Male: highly ornamented with a green head and crest patterned with white and black, rusty chest, white belly and red eyes

Juvenile: same as female

Nest: cavity; female lines old woodpecker cavity; 1 brood per year

Eggs: 10-15; creamy white, unmarked

Incubation: 28-36 days; female incubates

Fledging: 56-68 days; female teaches young to feed

Migration: complete, to southern states

Food: aquatic insects, plants, seeds

Compare: Smaller than the female Northern Shoveler (pg. 151) and lacks the long wide bill. Smaller than the female Mallard (pg. 161), which lacks Wood Duck's white eye ring.

Stan's Notes: A common duck of quiet, shallow backwater ponds. Nests in old woodpecker holes or in nest boxes. Often seen flying deep within a forest or perched high up on the branches of trees. Female takes flight with a loud squealing call and enters the nest cavity from full flight. Will lay eggs in a neighboring female nest (egg dumping), resulting in some clutches in excess of 20 eggs. Young remain in the nest cavity only 24 hours after hatching, then jump from up to 30 feet to ground or water to follow their mother. After that, they never return to the nest.

male pg. 217

female

NORTHERN SHOVELER
Anas clypeata

MIGRATION

Size: 20" (50 cm)

Female: Medium-sized brown duck speckled with black. Green speculum. An extraordinarily large spoon-shaped bill, almost always held pointed toward the water.

Male: same spoon-shaped bill, iridescent green head, rusty sides and white breast

Juvenile: same as female

Nest: ground; female builds; 1 brood per year

Eggs: 9-12; olive, unmarked

Incubation: 22-25 days; female incubates

Fledging: 30-60 days; female leads young to food

Migration: complete, to southern states and Central America

Food: aquatic insects, plants

Compare: Similar to female Mallard (pg. 161). Check for spoon-shaped bill. Larger size than the average female Wood Duck (pg. 149) and lacking the white eye ring.

Stan's Notes: One of several species of shoveler, so called because of the peculiarly shaped bill. The Northern Shoveler is the only species of these ducks in North America. Seen in small flocks of five to ten, swimming low in water with large bills always pointed toward water, as if they're too heavy to lift. More commonly seen during spring migration. Feeds primarily by filtering tiny plants and insects from the water's surface with bill.

151

soaring

RED-TAILED HAWK
Buteo jamaicensis

YEAR-ROUND

Size: 19-25" (48-63 cm); up to 4-foot wingspan

Male: Large hawk with amazing variety of colors from bird to bird, from chocolate brown to nearly all white. Often brown with a white breast and a distinctive brown belly band. Rust red tail usually only seen from above. Underside of wing is white with small dark patch on leading edge near shoulder.

Female: same as male, often larger

Juvenile: similar to adult, lacking a red tail, speckled chest

Nest: platform; male and female build; 1 brood per year

Eggs: 2-3; white, without markings or sometimes marked with brown

Incubation: 30-35 days; female and male incubate

Fledging: 45-46 days; male and female feed young

Migration: partial migrator, to southern states, a small percentage non-migrator

Food: mice, birds, snakes, insects

Compare: Red-shouldered Hawk (pg. 143) and Sharp-shinned Hawk (pg. 197) are much smaller.

Stan's Notes: A common hawk of open country and cities in the state, often seen perched on freeway light posts. Look for it circling above open fields, searching for prey. Their large stick nests are commonly seen along roads in large trees. Stick nests are lined with finer material such as evergreen needles. Will return to the same nest site each year. Doesn't develop red tail until second year.

153

BARRED OWL
Strix varia

YEAR-ROUND

Size: 20-24" (50-60 cm)

Male: A chunky brown and gray owl with a large head and dark brown eyes. Dark horizontal barring on chest, and vertical streaking on the belly.

Female: same as male, only slightly larger

Juvenile: same as adult

Nest: cavity; no nesting material is brought in; 1 brood per year

Eggs: 2-3; white, unmarked

Incubation: 28-33 days; female incubates

Fledging: 42-44 days; female and male feed young

Migration: non-migrator

Food: mammals, small birds

Compare: It's our only owl with dark eyes. Lacks the "horns" of the Great Horned Owl (pg. 157). About twice the size of the tiny Eastern Screech-Owl (pg. 191).

Stan's Notes: A very common owl that can often be seen hunting during the day. Prefers dense woodland with sparse undergrowth. Can be attracted by a simple nest box with a large opening, which is attached to a tree. The young will stay with the parents for up to four months after fledging. Often sounds like a dog barking just before giving an eight-hoot call that sounds like, "Who-cooks-for-you? Who-cooks-for-you?" The Great Horned Owl sounds like, "Hoo-hoo-hoo-hoooo!"

GREAT HORNED OWL
Bubo virginianus

YEAR-ROUND

Size: 20-25" (50-63 cm)

Male: A robust brown "horned" owl with bright yellow eyes and V-shaped white bib.

Female: same as male, only slightly larger

Juvenile: similar to adult

Nest: no nest; takes over the nests of crows, Great Blue Herons and hawks, or uses partial cavities; 1 brood per year

Eggs: 2; white, unmarked

Incubation: 26-30 days; female incubates

Fledging: 30-35 days; male and female feed young

Migration: non-migrator

Food: small mammals, birds, snakes, insects

Compare: The Barred Owl (pg. 155) has no "horns" and dark eyes. Over twice the size of the Eastern Screech-Owl (pg. 191).

Stan's Notes: The largest owl in the state. The earliest nesting bird in Kentucky, it lays eggs in January and February. Has excellent hearing; able to hear a mouse moving under a foot of snow. "Ears" are actually tufts of feathers (horns) and have nothing to do with hearing. Not able to turn head all the way around. Wing feathers are ragged on the end, resulting in a silent flight. Eyelids close from the top down, like humans. Fearless, it is one of the few animals that will kill skunks and porcupines. Because of this, sometimes it is called Flying Tiger.

male pg. 203

female

NORTHERN HARRIER
Circus cyaneus

WINTER

Size: 24" (60 cm)

Female: A slim, low-flying hawk. Dark brown back with brown-streaked breast and belly. Large white rump patch and narrow black bands across tail. Tips of wings black.

Male: silver gray with large white rump patch and white belly, faint narrow bands across tail, tips of wings black

Juvenile: similar to female, with orange breast

Nest: platform; female and male build; 1 brood per year

Eggs: 4-8; bluish white, unmarked

Incubation: 31-32 days; female incubates

Fledging: 30-35 days; male and female feed young

Migration: complete, to southern states and Central America

Food: mice, snakes

Compare: Slimmer than Red-tailed Hawk (pg. 153). Look for black bands on tail and a white rump patch.

Stan's Notes: One of the easiest hawks to identify. Harriers glide just above the ground, following the contours of the land while searching for prey. Wings are held just above the horizontal position, tilting back and forth in the wind, similar to Turkey Vultures. Was formerly called Marsh Hawk due to its habit of hunting over marshes. Nests on the ground. At all ages, the Northern Harrier has distinctive owl-like face disks.

male pg. 219

female

MALLARD
Anas platyrhynchos

Size: 27-28" (69-71 cm)

Female: All brown with orange and black bill. Small blue and white wing mark (speculum).

Male: large, bulbous green head, white necklace, rust brown or chestnut chest, combination of gray and white on sides, yellow bill, legs and feet

Juvenile: same as female, but with yellow bill

Nest: ground; female builds; 1 brood per year

Eggs: 7-10; greenish to whitish, unmarked

Incubation: 26-30 days; female incubates

Fledging: 42-52 days; female leads young to food

Migration: complete, to southern states, small percentage non-migrator

Food: seeds, plants, aquatic insects, will come to ground feeders offering corn

Compare: The female Northern Shoveler (pg. 151) is smaller and has a large spoon-shaped bill. The female Wood Duck (pg. 149) is smaller and has a white eye ring.

Stan's Notes: A familiar duck of lakes and ponds. Will return to place of birth. The name "Mallard" comes from the Latin *masculus*, meaning "male," referring to the habit of males not taking part in raising ducklings. Both male and female have white tails and white underwings. Black central tail feathers of male curl upward.

displaying male

non-displaying

female

WILD TURKEY
Meleagris gallopavo

Size: 36-48" (90-120 cm)

Male: Large, plump brown and bronze bird with striking blue and red bare head. Fan tail and long, straight black beard in center of chest. Spurs on legs.

Female: thinner and less striking than male, usually lacking breast beard

Juvenile: same as adult

Nest: ground; female builds; 1 brood per year

Eggs: 10-12; buff white with dull brown markings

Incubation: 27-28 days; female incubates

Fledging: 6-10 days; female leads young to food

Migration: non-migrator

Food: insects, seeds, fruit

Compare: This bird is distinctive and unlikely to be confused with others.

Stan's Notes: The largest game bird in the state, and the bird from which the domestic turkey was bred. Almost became our national bird, but lost by one vote to the Bald Eagle. Nearly eliminated from Kentucky by the turn of the twentieth century due to market hunting and loss of habitat. Restoration efforts began in the 1930s and continues today. Strong fliers, they can approach 60 mph. Able to fly straight up, then away. Eyesight three times better than humans. Hearing is also excellent; able to hear competing males up to a mile away. Males hold "harems" of up to 20 females. Males are known as toms, females are hens and the young are called poults. At night, they roost in trees.

RUBY-CROWNED KINGLET
Regulus calendula

WINTER

Size: 4" (10 cm)

Male: Small, teardrop-shaped green-to-gray bird. Two white wing bars. Hidden ruby-colored crown. White eye ring.

Female: same as male, lacks ruby crown

Juvenile: same as adult

Nest: pendulous; female builds; 1 brood per year

Eggs: 4-5; white with brown markings

Incubation: 11-12 days; female incubates

Fledging: 11-12 days; female and male feed young

Migration: complete, to southern states, Mexico and Central America

Food: insects, berries

Compare: Similar to the Golden-crowned Kinglet (pg. 167), but crown is ruby colored.

Stan's Notes: The second smallest bird in the state, it takes a quick eye to see the male's ruby crown. Most commonly seen during the spring and autumn migrations, look for it flitting around thick shrubs low to the ground. Builds an unusual pendulous (sac-like) nest, intricately woven and decorated on the outside with colored lichens and mosses stuck together with spider webs. The nest is suspended from a branch overlapped by leaves, usually hung high in mature trees. The name "Kinglet" comes from the Anglo-Saxon *cyning*, or "king," referring to its ruby crown, and the diminutive suffix "let," meaning "small."

GOLDEN-CROWNED KINGLET
Regulus satrapa

WINTER

Size: 4" (10 cm)

Male: Tiny, plump green-to-gray bird. Distinctive yellow and orange patch with black border on the crown. A white eyebrow mark. Two white wing bars.

Female: same as male, but has a yellow crown, lacks any orange

Juvenile: same as adult

Nest: pendulous; female builds; 1-2 broods a year

Eggs: 5-9; white or creamy with brown markings

Incubation: 14-15 days; female incubates

Fledging: 14-19 days; female and male feed young

Migration: complete, to southern states, Mexico and Central America

Food: insects, fruit, tree sap

Compare: Similar to Ruby-crowned Kinglet (pg. 165), but Golden-crowned has an obvious crown. Smaller than the female American Goldfinch (pg. 245), which lacks any crown marking.

Stan's Notes: Common during winter in Kentucky, but might be more frequently seen during migration when flocks are moving through the state. Often seen in flocks that include chickadees, nuthatches, woodpeckers, Brown Creepers and Ruby-crowned Kinglets. Has a habit of flicking its wings when moving around. Unusual hanging nest is often made of moss, lichens and spider webs, and lined with bark and feathers. Can have so many eggs in its small nest that eggs are in two layers. Drinks tree sap and feeds by gleaning insects from trees. Can be very tame and approachable.

RED-BREASTED NUTHATCH
Sitta canadensis

Size: 4½" (11 cm)

Male: A small gray-backed bird with a black cap and a prominent eye line. A rust red breast and belly.

Female: gray cap, pale undersides

Juvenile: same as female

Nest: cavity; female builds; 1 brood per year

Eggs: 5-6; white with red brown markings

Incubation: 11-12 days; female incubates

Fledging: 14-20 days; female and male feed young

Migration: irruptive, moves around the state in search of food

Food: insects, seeds, visits seed and suet feeders

Compare: Smaller than the White-breasted Nuthatch (pg. 173), has a red breast instead of white.

Stan's Notes: Common during some winters and scarce in others, Red-breasted Nuthatch behaves like the White-breasted Nuthatch, climbing down tree trunks headfirst. Similar to chickadees, visits seed feeders, quickly grabbing a seed and flying off to crack it open. Will wedge a seed into a crevice and pound it open with several sharp blows. The name "Nuthatch" comes from the Middle English moniker *nuthak*, referring to the bird's habit of wedging a seed into a crevice and hacking it open. Look for it in mature conifers, frequently extracting seeds from cones. Doesn't excavate a cavity as the chickadee might; rather, it takes over a former woodpecker or chickadee cavity.

CAROLINA CHICKADEE
Poecile carolinensis

YEAR-ROUND

Size: 5" (13 cm)

Male: Mostly gray bird with a black cap and chin. White face and chest with tan belly. Darker gray tail.

Female: same as male

Juvenile: same as adult

Nest: cavity; female and male build or excavate; 1-2 broods per year

Eggs: 5-7; white with reddish brown markings

Incubation: 11-12 days; female and male incubate

Fledging: 13-17 days; female and male feed young

Migration: non-migrator

Food: insects, seeds, fruit, comes to seed and suet feeders

Compare: The Tufted Titmouse (pg. 181) has an erect crest, and lacks the black cap and chin.

Stan's Notes: A common bird of Kentucky. Can be attracted with a nest box with a 1¼-inch entrance hole. Female will give a loud snake-like hiss when disturbed on the nest. Often seen with other birds (mixed flock) during the winter. A friendly bird that can be tamed and hand fed. The Carolina Chickadee's song is a high, fast "chicka-dee-dee-dee-dee."

WHITE-BREASTED NUTHATCH
Sitta carolinensis

YEAR-ROUND

Size: 5-6" (13-15 cm)

Male: Slate gray with a white face and belly, and black cap and nape. Long thin bill, slightly upturned. Chestnut undertail.

Female: similar to male, gray cap and nape

Juvenile: same as adult

Nest: cavity; the female and male build; 1 brood per year

Eggs: 5-7; white with brown markings

Incubation: 11-12 days; female incubates

Fledging: 13-14 days; female and male feed young

Migration: non-migrator

Food: insects, seeds, visits seed and suet feeders

Compare: The Red-breasted Nuthatch (pg. 169) is smaller, and has rusty belly and distinctive black eye line.

Stan's Notes: The nuthatch's habit of hopping headfirst down tree trunks helps them see insects and eggs that birds climbing up the trunk might miss. Incredible climbing agility comes from an extra long hind toe claw or nail, nearly twice the size of front toe claws. The name "Nuthatch" comes from the Middle English moniker *nuthak*, referring to the bird's habit of wedging a seed into a crevice and hacking it open. Often seen in mixed flocks of chickadees, Brown Creepers and Downy Woodpeckers. Mated pairs remain together all year, defending small territories. Listen for its characteristic springtime call, "whi-whi-whi-whi," given in February and March. One of 17 worldwide nuthatch species.

male

female

YELLOW-RUMPED WARBLER
Dendroica coronata

WINTER

Size:	5-6" (13-15 cm)
Male:	Slate gray bird with black streaks on breast. Yellow patch on the head, flanks and rump. White chin and belly. Two white wing bars.
Female:	similar to male, duller color, mostly brown and white with matching yellow patches
Juvenile:	similar to female
Nest:	cup; female builds; 2 broods per year
Eggs:	4-5; white with brown markings
Incubation:	12-13 days; female incubates
Fledging:	10-12 days; female and male feed young
Migration:	complete, to southern states, Mexico and Central America
Food:	insects, berries, rarely comes to suet feeders
Compare:	Similar to other warblers, look for a combination of yellow patches on head, flanks and rump. Magnolia Warbler (pg. 251) is more yellow than Yellow-rumped Warbler. Prairie Warbler (pg. 255) has olive back with chestnut-colored streaks. Common Yellowthroat (pg. 247) has yellow breast, compared with Yellow-rumped Warbler's spots of yellow.

Stan's Notes: One of the most common warblers, seen in flocks of hundreds during spring and fall migrations, and one of the few warblers to spend the winter in Kentucky. Formerly called Myrtle Warbler. Sometimes called Butter-butts due to the yellow patch on rump. Males molt to a dull color similar to females each winter, retaining yellow patches. Familiar call is a robust "chip."

YELLOW-THROATED WARBLER
Dendroica dominica

SUMMER

Size: 5½" (14 cm)

Male: A gray-backed warbler with a bright yellow throat. Black streaks on white belly. A white spot on neck and white eyebrows.

Female: same as male, but duller with browner back

Juvenile: similar to female

Nest: cup; the female and male build; 1-2 broods per year

Eggs: 4-5; gray with dark markings

Incubation: 12-13 days; female incubates

Fledging: 10-12 days; female and male feed young

Migration: complete, to Central and South America

Food: insects

Compare: Similar to the Magnolia Warbler (pg. 251), but has a white belly with black streaks, compared with the black-streaked yellow belly of the Magnolia. Yellow-throated is a resident nester, while Magnolia is a migrant passing through the state.

Stan's Notes: One of the most widespread of Kentucky's nesting warblers. Among the first returning warblers to the state, usually around mid-April. Prefers cypress and oak woodland. Finds food by creeping along and searching under vertical surfaces such as tree bark. Highly attracted to water, is often seen bathing in any puddle of water. In some, the white eyebrows are tinged yellow. It is rarely a Brown-headed Cowbird host.

female pg. 81

male

DARK-EYED JUNCO
Junco hyemalis

YEAR-ROUND
WINTER

Size: 5½" (14 cm)

Male: A round, dark-eyed bird with slate-gray-to-charcoal chest, head and back. White belly. Pink bill. Since the outermost tail feathers are white, tail appears as a white V in flight.

Female: same as male, only tan-to-brown color

Juvenile: similar to female, but has a streaked chest and head

Nest: cup; female and male build; 2 broods a year

Eggs: 3-5; white with reddish brown markings

Incubation: 12-13 days; female incubates

Fledging: 10-13 days; male and female feed young

Migration: complete, all across the U.S.

Food: seeds, insects, will come to seed feeders

Compare: Rarely confused with any other bird. Large flocks come to feed under bird feeders.

Stan's Notes: A common winter bird of Kentucky. Usually seen on the ground in small flocks. Migrates from Canada to Kentucky and beyond. Females tend to migrate farther south than males. Look for white outer tail feathers that flash in flight. Several junco species have now been combined into one, simply called Dark-eyed Junco. Most comfortable on the ground, juncos will "double-scratch" with both feet to expose seeds and insects. Consumes many weed seeds. A flocking bird, it adheres to a rigid social hierarchy with dominant birds chasing less dominant birds.

TUFTED TITMOUSE
Baeolophus bicolor

Size: 6" (15 cm)

Male: Slate gray bird with a white chest and belly. Pointed crest. Flanks are washed in a rusty brown. Gray legs and dark eyes.

Female: same as male

Juvenile: same as adult

Nest: cavity, takes over former woodpecker hole; female builds; 2 broods per year

Eggs: 5-7; white with brown markings

Incubation: 13-14 days; female incubates

Fledging: 15-18 days; female and male feed young

Migration: non-migrator

Food: insects, seeds, fruit, will come to seed and suet feeders

Compare: Closely related to, but slightly larger than, the Carolina Chickadee (pg. 171). The Chickadee lacks the crest of the Titmouse. Similar in size and color to White-breasted Nuthatch (pg. 173), but Nuthatch doesn't have a crest.

Stan's Notes: Is well known for its quickly repeated "peter-peter-peter" call. Prefix "Tit" comes from a Scandinavian word meaning "little." Suffix "mouse" is derived from the Old English word *mase*, meaning "bird." Simply translated, it is "a small bird." Notorious for pulling hair from sleeping dogs, cats and squirrels to line their nests. Attracted with nest boxes. Usually seen only one or two at a time. Male feeds female during courtship and nesting.

EASTERN PHOEBE
Sayornis phoebe

SUMMER

Size: 7" (18 cm)

Male: Gray bird with dark wings, light olive green belly and a thin dark bill.

Female: same as male

Juvenile: same as adult

Nest: cup; female builds; 2 broods per year

Eggs: 4-5; white, unmarked

Incubation: 15-16 days; female incubates

Fledging: 15-16 days; male and female feed young

Migration: complete, to southern states and Mexico

Food: insects

Compare: Like most other olive gray birds, it is hard to distinguish identifying markings. Eastern Phoebe lacks any white eye ring. Easier to identify by well-enunciated song, "fee-bee," or characteristic of hawking for insects.

Stan's Notes: A sparrow-sized bird often seen on the end of a dead branch. It sits waiting for a passing insect, flies out to catch it and then returns to the same branch, a process called hawking. Has a habit of pumping and spreading its tail when perched. Will build nest under the eaves of a house, under a bridge or in culverts. The nest, made of mud, grass and moss, is lined with hair and feathers. The name is derived from its characteristic song, "fee-bee," which is repeated over and over from the tops of dead branches.

EASTERN KINGBIRD
Tyrannus tyrannus

SUMMER

Size: 8" (20 cm)

Male: Mostly black gray bird with white belly and chin. Black head and tail with a distinctive white band across the end of the tail. Has a concealed red crown that is rarely seen.

Female: same as male

Juvenile: same as adult

Nest: cup; male and female build; 1 brood a year

Eggs: 3-4; white with brown markings

Incubation: 16-18 days; female incubates

Fledging: 16-18 days; female and male feed young

Migration: complete, to Central and South America

Food: insects, fruit

Compare: Rarely confused with other birds. Medium-sized bird, smaller than American Robin (pg. 193). Look for the white band along the end of the tail to identify.

Stan's Notes: A common bird of open fields and prairies. Acting unafraid of other birds and chasing the larger ones, it is perceived as having an attitude. Bold behavior gave rise to its common name, King. Perches on tall branches, watching for insects. After flying out to catch them, returns to the same perch, a technique called hawking. Male and female return to mating ground and defend a territory together.

GREAT CRESTED FLYCATCHER
Myiarchus crinitus

Size: 8" (20 cm)

Male: Gray head with prominent crest. Gray back and throat with bright yellow belly, yellow extending under reddish brown tail. Lower bill is yellow at base.

Female: same as male

Juvenile: same as adult

Nest: cavity; the female and male build; 1 brood per year

Eggs: 4-6; white or buff with brown markings

Incubation: 13-15 days; female incubates

Fledging: 14-21 days; female and male feed young

Migration: complete, to Mexico and Central America

Food: insects, fruit

Compare: The Eastern Kingbird (pg. 185) has a white band across the tail. Similar to the Eastern Phoebe (pg. 183), but the Flycatcher has an obvious crest and yellow belly.

Stan's Notes: Breeds mostly in western Kentucky. A common bird of almost any wooded area, it lives high up in trees, rarely coming to the ground. Often heard before seen. Feeds by gleaning insects from the leaves of trees. Nests in old woodpecker holes, but can be attracted to a nest box placed high up in a tree with an entrance hole of 1½ -2½ inches. Often stuffs its nest with a collection of fur, feathers, string and snakeskins.

GRAY CATBIRD
Dumetella carolinensis

Size: 9" (22.5 cm)

Male: Handsome slate-gray bird with black crown and a long, thin black bill. Often seen with its tail lifted, exposing a chestnut-colored patch under tail.

Female: same as male

Juvenile: same as adult

Nest: cup; female and male build; 2 broods a year

Eggs: 4-6; blue green, unmarked

Incubation: 12-13 days; female incubates

Fledging: 10-11 days; female and male feed young

Migration: complete, to southern states

Food: insects, fruit

Compare: Larger than Eastern Phoebe (pg. 183), it lacks the Phoebe's olive belly. Similar size as Eastern Kingbird (pg. 185), but it lacks the Kingbird's white belly and white tail band.

Stan's Notes: A secretive bird that the Chippewa Indians named Bird That Cries With Grief due to its raspy call. The call sounds like a house cat's mewing, hence its common name. It often mimics other birds, rarely repeating the same phrases. Will only nest in thick shrubs and is more often heard than seen. Quickly flies back into the shrubs when approached. If a cowbird introduces an egg into a catbird nest, the catbird will quickly break it, then eject it.

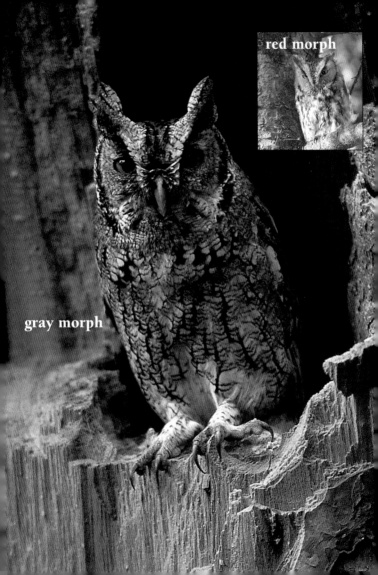

red morph

gray morph

EASTERN SCREECH-OWL
Megascops asio

Size: 9" (22.5 cm)

Male: Small "eared" owl that occurs in one of two permanent color morphs. Is either mottled with gray and white, or is red brown (rust) with white. Bright yellow eyes.

Female: same as male

Juvenile: lighter gray than adult, may lack ear tufts

Nest: cavity; former woodpecker cavity; 1 brood per year

Eggs: 4-5; white, unmarked

Incubation: 25-26 days; female incubates, male feeds female during incubation

Fledging: 26-27 days; male and female feed young

Migration: non-migrator

Food: large insects, small mammals, birds, snakes

Compare: The only small owl in the state with ear tufts. Can be gray or rust-colored.

Stan's Notes: A common owl active at dusk and during the night. Excellent hearing and eyesight. Seldom gives a screeching call; more commonly gives a tremulous, descending whiny trill that sounds like it came from the sound track of a scary movie. Will nest in a wooden nest box. Often seen sunning themselves at nest box holes during the winter. Male and female may roost together at night, and are thought to mate for life. Different colorations are called morphs. The gray morph is more common than the red.

male

female

AMERICAN ROBIN
Turdus migratorius

YEAR-ROUND

Size: 9-11" (22.5-28 cm)

Male: A familiar gray bird with a rusty red chest, a nearly black head and tail, and black streaks on white chin. White eye ring.

Female: similar to male, but has a gray head and a duller chest

Juvenile: similar to female, but has a speckled chest and brown back

Nest: cup; female builds with help from the male; 2-3 broods per year

Eggs: 4-7; pale blue, unmarked

Incubation: 12-14 days; female incubates

Fledging: 14-16 days; female and male feed young

Migration: complete, to southern states and Central America, small percentage non-migrator

Food: insects, fruit, berries, worms

Compare: Familiar bird to all.

Stan's Notes: Although they can be seen year-round, many of Kentucky's robins will migrate to southern states. Most return by late February and are nesting by March. Can be heard singing all night long in spring. Most people don't realize how easy it is to tell the difference between the male and female robin. Look for the male's dark, nearly black head and brick-red chest, compared with the female's gray head and dull red chest. Robins are not listening for worms when they cock their heads to one side or the other. They are looking with eyes that are placed far back on the sides of their heads. A very territorial bird. Often seen fighting its own reflection in windows.

displaying

NORTHERN MOCKINGBIRD
Mimus polyglottos

YEAR-ROUND

Size: 10" (25 cm)

Male: Silvery gray head and back with light gray chest and belly. White wing patches, seen in flight or during display. Tail mostly black with white outer tail feathers. Black bill.

Female: same as male

Juvenile: overall dull gray, a heavily streaked chest, gray bill

Nest: cup; female and male build; 2 broods per year, sometimes more

Eggs: 3-5; blue green with brown markings

Incubation: 12-13 days; female incubates

Fledging: 11-13 days; female and male feed young

Migration: partial migrator in northern states

Food: insects, fruit

Compare: The Gray Catbird (pg. 189) is a slate gray and lacks the Mockingbird's wing patches. Look for Mockingbird to spread its wings, flash its white wing patches and wag its tail from side to side.

Stan's Notes: Very animated, male and female perform elaborate mating dances by facing each other, heads and tails erect. They run toward each other, flashing white wing patches, and then retreat to nearby cover. Thought to also flash wing patches to scare up insects when hunting. Known to imitate other birds (vocal mimicry), hence its common name. Young males often sing at night.

soaring

SHARP-SHINNED HAWK
Accipiter striatus

Size: 10-14" (25-36 cm)

Male: Small woodland hawk with gray back and head, and rusty red breast. Long tail with several dark tail bands, widest band at end of squared-off tail. Red eyes.

Female: same as male, only larger

Juvenile: same size as adult, with a brown back and heavily streaked breast, yellow eyes

Nest: platform; female builds; 1 brood per year

Eggs: 4-5; white with brown markings

Incubation: 32-35 days; female incubates

Fledging: 24-27 days; female and male feed young

Migration: complete, to southern states, Mexico and Central America

Food: birds, small mammals

Compare: Nearly identical to Cooper's Hawk (pg. 201), only smaller. Look for squared end of tail on the Sharp-shinned, compared with the round end of Cooper's. Smaller than the Red-shouldered Hawk (pg. 143), which lacks Sharp-shinned's gray back.

Stan's Notes: A common hawk of backyards and woodland, often seen swooping in on birds visiting feeders. Short rounded wings and long tail allow this hawk to navigate through thick stands of trees in pursuit of prey. Common name comes from the sharp keel on the leading edge of its "shin," although it is actually below rather than above the bird's ankle on the tarsus bone of foot. The tarsus in most birds is round. In flight, head doesn't protrude as far as the head of the Cooper's Hawk.

ROCK PIGEON
Columba livia

YEAR-ROUND

Size: 13" (33 cm)

Male: No set color pattern. Gray to white, patches of iridescent greens and blues, usually with a light rump patch.

Female: same as male

Juvenile: same as adult

Nest: platform; female builds; 3-4 broods a year

Eggs: 1-2; white, unmarked

Incubation: 18-20 days; female and male incubate

Fledging: 25-26 days; female and male feed young

Migration: non-migrator

Food: seeds

Compare: Larger than light-brown-colored Mourning Dove (pg. 131).

Stan's Notes: Also known as Domestic Pigeon, it was introduced to North America from Europe by the early settlers. Most common around cities and barnyards, where it scratches for seeds. The wide color variation comes from years of selective breeding while in captivity. Parents feed young a regurgitated liquid called crop-milk the first few days of life. One of the few birds that can drink without tilting its head back. Nests under bridges, on buildings, balconies, barns and sheds. Once poisoned as a "nuisance city bird," many cities have Peregrine Falcons that feed on Rock Pigeons, keeping their numbers in check.

soaring

COOPER'S HAWK
Accipiter cooperii

YEAR-ROUND

Size: 14-20" (36-50 cm)

Male: A medium hawk with short wings and a long rounded tail with several black bands. Rusty chest and dark wing tips. Slate gray back. Bright yellow spot at base of gray bill (cere). Red eyes.

Female: similar to male, only slightly larger

Juvenile: brown back with brown streaks on chest, yellow eyes

Nest: platform; male and female build; 1 brood per year

Eggs: 2-4; greenish with brown markings

Incubation: 32-36 days; female and male incubate

Fledging: 28-32 days; male and female feed young

Migration: non-migrator to partial migrator, southern states and Mexico

Food: small birds, mammals

Compare: Nearly identical to the Sharp-shinned Hawk (pg. 197), only larger, darker gray and with a rounded-off tail.

Stan's Notes: A common hawk of the woodland. In flight, look for its large head, short wings and proportionately long tail. Short stubby wings help it maneuver between trees while pursuing small birds. Will come to feeders, hunting for unaware birds. Flies with long glides followed by a few quick flaps. Known to ambush prey, it will fly into heavy brush or even run on the ground in pursuit. Nestlings have gray eyes that become bright yellow at one year and later, dark red.

male

female pg. 159

NORTHERN HARRIER
Circus cyaneus

WINTER

Size: 24" (60 cm)

Male: A slim, low-flying hawk. Silver gray with a large white rump patch and a white belly. Faint narrow bands across the tail. Tips of wings black.

Female: dark brown back, a brown-streaked breast and belly, large white rump patch, narrow black bands across tail, tips of wings black

Juvenile: similar to female, with orange breast

Nest: platform; female and male build; 1 brood per year

Eggs: 4-8; bluish white, unmarked

Incubation: 31-32 days; female incubates

Fledging: 30-35 days; male and female feed young

Migration: complete, to southern states and Central America

Food: mice, snakes

Compare: Slimmer than Red-tailed Hawk (pg. 153). Look for black bands on tail and a white rump patch.

Stan's Notes: One of the easiest hawks to identify. Harriers glide just above the ground, following the contours of the land while searching for prey. Wings are held just above the horizontal position, tilting back and forth in the wind, similar to Turkey Vultures. Was formerly called Marsh Hawk due to its habit of hunting over marshes. Nests on the ground. At all ages, the Northern Harrier has distinctive owl-like face disks.

CANADA GOOSE
Branta canadensis

Size: 25-43" (63-109 cm)

Male: Large gray goose with black neck and head, with a white chin or cheek strap.

Female: same as male

Juvenile: same as adult

Nest: platform; female builds; 1 brood per year

Eggs: 5-10; white, unmarked

Incubation: 25-30 days; female incubates

Fledging: 42-55 days; male and female teach young to feed

Migration: non-migrator

Food: aquatic plants, insects, seeds

Compare: A large goose that is hardly ever confused with any other bird.

Stan's Notes: Introduced into several parts of Kentucky, they are now breeding in the state and are common year-round residents. Once not too common, they adapted to our changed environment very well. Adults will mate for many years, and will only start to breed in their third year. Males often act as sentinels, standing on the edge of the group and bobbing their heads up and down, becoming very aggressive to anyone who approaches. Will hiss as if to display displeasure. Adults molt primary flight feathers while raising young, rendering family groups flightless at the same time. Several subspecies vary geographically around the U.S. Generally they are paler in color in eastern groups, and darker in western. Their size decreases northward, with the smallest subspecies found on the Arctic tundra.

SANDHILL CRANE
Grus canadensis

MIGRATION

Size: 40-48" (102-120 cm); up to 7-foot wingspan

Male: Elegant gray bird with long legs and neck. Wings and body often stained rusty brown. Scarlet red cap. Red eyes.

Female: same as male

Juvenile: dull brown without red cap, yellow eyes

Nest: platform, on the ground; female and male build; 1 brood per year

Eggs: 2; olive with brown markings

Incubation: 28-32 days; female and male incubate

Fledging: 65 days; female and male feed young

Migration: complete, to southern states and Mexico

Food: insects, fruit, worms, plants, amphibians

Compare: Similar size as Great Blue Heron (pg. 209), but Crane has a shorter bill and a red patch on head. The Great Blue Heron flies with its neck held in an S shape, unlike the Crane's straight neck.

Stan's Notes: Among the tallest birds in the world and capable of flying at great heights. Usually seen in large undisturbed fields near water. Often heard before seen, they have a very distinctive rattling call. Plumage often appears rust brown because of staining from mud during preening. Characteristic flight with upstroke quicker than down. For their spectacular mating dance the performers face each other, bow and jump into the air while uttering a loud cackling sound and flapping wings. Often flips sticks and grass into the air during dance.

GREAT BLUE HERON
Ardea herodias

YEAR-ROUND MIGRATION

Size: 42-52" (107-132 cm)

Male: Tall gray heron. Black eyebrows extend into several long plumes off the back of head. Long yellow bill. Feathers at base of neck drop down in a kind of necklace.

Female: same as male

Juvenile: same as adult, but more brown than gray, with a black crown and no plumes

Nest: platform; male and female build; 1 brood per year

Eggs: 3-5; blue green, unmarked

Incubation: 27-28 days; female and male incubate

Fledging: 56-60 days; male and female feed young

Migration: complete, to southern states, Central and South America

Food: small fish, frogs, insects, snakes

Compare: Similar size as the Sandhill Crane (pg. 207), but lacks the Crane's red crown. Crane flies with neck held straight, unlike the Heron's S-shaped neck.

Stan's Notes: One of the most common herons, it often barks like a dog when startled. Seen stalking small fish in shallow water. Will strike at mice, squirrels and just about anything else it might come across. Flies holding neck in an S shape, with its long legs trailing straight out behind. The wings are held in cupped fashion during flight. Nests in colonies of up to 100 birds. Nests in treetops near or over open water.

male

female

RUBY-THROATED HUMMINGBIRD
Archilochus colubris

SUMMER

Size: 3-3½" (7.5-9 cm)

Male: Tiny iridescent green bird with black throat patch that reflects bright ruby red in sun.

Female: same as male, lacking throat patch

Juvenile: same as female

Nest: cup; female builds; 1-2 broods per year

Eggs: 2; white, unmarked

Incubation: 12-14 days; female incubates

Fledging: 14-18 days; female feeds young

Migration: complete, to southern states, Mexico and Central America

Food: nectar, insects

Compare: No other bird is as tiny. The Sphinx Moth hovers at flowers like the Hummingbird, but has clear wings and a mouth part that looks like a straw, which coils up when not at a flower. Moves much slower than the Hummingbird and can be approached.

Stan's Notes: The smallest bird in the state. Able to hover, fly up and down, and is the only bird to fly backward. Does not sing, but will chatter or buzz to communicate. The wings create a humming noise, flapping 50 to 60 times per second or faster during chasing flights. Weighing just 2 to 3 grams, it takes about five average-sized hummingbirds to equal the weight of a single chickadee. The heart beats at an incredible 1,260 times a minute and it breathes 250 times a minute. Constructs its nest with plant material and spider webs, gluing pieces of lichen on the outside of nest for camouflage. Attracted to tubular red flowers.

male

female pg. 149

WOOD DUCK
Aix sponsa

SUMMER
WINTER

Size: 17-20" (43-50 cm)

Male: A small, highly ornamented dabbling duck with a green head and crest patterned with white and black. A rusty chest, white belly and red eyes.

Female: brown, similar size and shape to male, has bright white eye ring and a not-so-obvious crest, blue patch on wing often hidden

Juvenile: same as female

Nest: cavity; female lines old woodpecker cavity; 1 brood per year

Eggs: 10-15; creamy white, unmarked

Incubation: 28-36 days; female incubates

Fledging: 56-68 days; female teaches young to feed

Migration: complete, to southern states

Food: aquatic insects, plants, seeds

Compare: Smaller than the male Northern Shoveler (pg. 217). Lacks Shoveler's long wide bill.

Stan's Notes: A common duck of quiet, shallow backwater ponds. Nearly extinct around 1900 due to over-hunting, but is doing well now. Nests in old woodpecker holes or nest boxes. Often seen flying deep within a forest or perched high up on branches of trees. Female takes flight with a loud squealing call and enters the nest cavity from full flight. Will lay eggs in a neighboring female nest (egg dumping), resulting in some clutches in excess of 20 eggs. Young remain in the nest cavity only 24 hours after hatching, then jump from up to 30 feet to ground or water to follow their mother. After that, they never return to the nest.

GREEN HERON
Butorides virescens

Size: 16-22" (40-56 cm)

Male: Short stocky heron with a blue-green back, and rusty red neck and chest. Dark green crest. Short legs, normally yellow, but turn bright orange during breeding season.

Female: same as male

Juvenile: similar to adult, with a blue-gray back and white-streaked chest and neck

Nest: platform; female and male build; 2 broods per year

Eggs: 2-4; light green, unmarked

Incubation: 21-25 days; female and male incubate

Fledging: 35-36 days; female and male feed young

Migration: complete, to South America

Food: fish, insects, aquatic plants

Compare: Much smaller than the Great Blue Heron (pg. 209). Look for a small heron with dark green back stalking lakeshores.

Stan's Notes: Often gives an explosive, rasping "skyew" call when startled. Sometimes it looks like it doesn't have a neck, because it holds its head close to its body. Hunts for fish and aquatic insects by waiting along a shore or wades stealthily. Has been known to place an object, such as an insect, on the water surface to attract fish to catch. Has a crest that it raises when excited.

male

female pg. 151

NORTHERN SHOVELER
Anas clypeata

MIGRATION

Size: 20" (50 cm)

Male: Medium-sized duck with iridescent green head, rusty sides and white breast. Has an extraordinarily large spoon-shaped bill that is almost always held pointed toward water.

Female: same spoon-shaped bill, brown and black all over and green speculum

Juvenile: same as female

Nest: ground; female builds; 1 brood per year

Eggs: 9-12; olive, unmarked

Incubation: 22-25 days; female incubates

Fledging: 30-60 days; female leads young to food

Migration: complete, to southern states and Central America

Food: aquatic insects, plants

Compare: Similar to the male Mallard (pg. 219), but Shoveler has a large, characteristic spoon-shaped bill. Larger than the average male Wood Duck (pg. 213) and lacks the Wood Duck's crest.

Stan's Notes: One of several species of shoveler, so called because of the peculiarly shaped bill. The Northern Shoveler is the only species of these ducks in North America. Seen in small flocks of five to ten, swimming low in water with large bills always pointed toward water, as if they're too heavy to lift. More commonly seen during spring migration. Feeds primarily by filtering tiny plants and insects from the water's surface with bill.

female pg. 161

male

MALLARD
Anas platyrhynchos

YEAR-ROUND
WINTER

Size: 27-28" (69-71 cm)

Male: Large, bulbous green head, white necklace and rust brown or chestnut-colored chest. A combination of gray and white on sides. Yellow bill, legs and feet.

Female: all brown with orange and black bill, small blue and white wing mark (speculum)

Juvenile: same as female, but with yellow bill

Nest: ground; female builds; 1 brood per year

Eggs: 7-10; greenish to whitish, unmarked

Incubation: 26-30 days; female incubates

Fledging: 42-52 days; female leads young to food

Migration: complete, to southern states, small percentage non-migrator

Food: seeds, plants, aquatic insects, will come to ground feeders offering corn

Compare: The male Northern Shoveler (pg. 217) has a white chest with rust on sides and dark spoon-shaped bill.

Stan's Notes: A familiar duck of lakes and ponds. Will return to place of birth. The name "Mallard" comes from the Latin *masculus*, meaning "male," referring to the habit of males not taking part in raising ducklings. Both male and female have white tails and white underwings. Black central tail feathers of male curl upward.

male

female pg. 243

AMERICAN REDSTART
Setophaga ruticilla

MIGRATION
SUMMER

Size: 5" (13 cm)

Male: Small, striking black bird with contrasting patches of orange on sides, wings and tail. White belly.

Female: olive brown with yellow patches instead of the male's orange, white belly

Juvenile: same as female, the juvenile male is tinged orange for first year

Nest: cup; female builds; 1 brood per year

Eggs: 3-5; off-white with brown markings

Incubation: 12 days; female incubates

Fledging: 9 days; female and male feed young

Migration: complete, to Mexico, Central America and South America

Food: insects, seeds, berries rarely

Compare: Male Red-winged Blackbird (pg. 9) and the male Baltimore Oriole (pg. 223) are much larger at roughly 8 inches. The only small black and orange bird flitting around tops of trees.

Stan's Notes: A common and widespread warbler in Kentucky, mostly seen during spring migration. Prefers large unbroken tracts of forest. Appears to be hyperactive when feeding, hovering and darting back and forth to glean insects from the leaves. Look for flashing black and orange color high in the trees. Often droops its wings and fans its tail just before launching out to catch an insect.

221

male

female pg. 259

BALTIMORE ORIOLE
Icterus galbula

MIGRATION
SUMMER

Size: 7-8" (18-20 cm)

Male: Bright flaming-orange bird with black head and black extending down nape of neck onto the back. Black wings with white and orange wing bars. An orange tail with black streaks. Gray bill and dark eyes.

Female: pale yellow with orange tones, gray brown wings, white wing bars, gray bill, dark eyes

Juvenile: same as female

Nest: pendulous; female builds; 1 brood per year

Eggs: 4-5; bluish with brown markings

Incubation: 12-14 days; female incubates

Fledging: 12-14 days; female and male feed young

Migration: complete, to Mexico, Central America and South America

Food: insects, fruit, nectar, comes to orange half and nectar feeders

Compare: The male Orchard Oriole (pg. 225) is much darker orange than the Baltimore's flaming orange. Male American Redstart (pg. 221) is smaller and has more black than orange.

Stan's Notes: A fantastic songster, this bird is often heard before seen. Easily attracted to a feeder offering grape jelly, orange halves or sugar water (nectar). Parents bring young to feeders. Sits in tops of trees feeding on caterpillars. Female builds sock-like nest at the outermost branches of tall trees. Often returns to the same area year after year. Some of the last birds to arrive in spring (April) and first to leave in fall (August).

female pg. 261

male

ORCHARD ORIOLE
Icterus spurius

MIGRATION
SUMMER

Size: 7-8" (18-20 cm)

Male: Dull orange bird with black head and black extending down the back. A black chin, tail and wings. Single white wing bars. A long, thin black bill with a small gray mark on lower mandible (jaw).

Female: olive green back with dull yellow belly, two white wing bars on dark gray wings

Juvenile: same as female, first-year male has a black bib

Nest: pendulous; female builds; 1 brood per year

Eggs: 3-5; pale blue to white, brown markings

Incubation: 11-12 days; female and male incubate

Fledging: 11-14 days; female and male feed young

Migration: complete, to central Mexico and northern South America

Food: insects, fruit, comes to fruit/nectar feeders

Compare: Similar to male Baltimore Oriole (pg. 223), but the male Orchard Oriole has a much darker orange body.

Stan's Notes: Prefers orchards and open woods, hence its common name. Eats insects until wild fruit starts to ripen. One of the last birds to arrive in spring and one of the first to leave each fall, spending only about four to five months in Kentucky. Usually nests alone, but sometimes in small colonies. Parents bring the young to jelly and orange half feeders shortly after fledging. Many people mistakenly think the orioles have left during summer but, in fact, the birds are concentrating on finding insects to feed their young.

female pg. 71

male

HOUSE FINCH
Carpodacus mexicanus

YEAR-ROUND

Size: 5" (13 cm)

Male: An orange red face, chest and rump, with brown cap. Brown marking behind eyes. Brown wings streaked with white. A white belly with brown streaks.

Female: brown with heavily streaked white chest

Juvenile: similar to female

Nest: cup, sometimes in cavities; female builds; 2 broods per year

Eggs: 4-5; pale blue, lightly marked

Incubation: 12-14 days; female incubates

Fledging: 15-19 days; female and male feed young

Migration: non-migrator to partial migrator, will move around to find food

Food: seeds, fruit, leaf buds, will visit seed feeders

Compare: Male Purple Finch (pg. 229) is very similar, but male House Finch lacks the red cap. Look for the streaked chest and belly, and brown cap of male House Finch.

Stan's Notes: A relatively new bird to Kentucky (first reported in the early 1970s and first nests reported by 1981), it was originally introduced to Long Island, New York, in the 1940s from western America. A very social bird, it visits feeders in small flocks. Seems to prefer nesting in hanging flower baskets. Incubating female is fed by male. Loud and cheerful warbling song. The House Finch suffers from a fatal eye disease that causes the eyes to crust over.

female pg. 85

male

PURPLE FINCH
Carpodacus purpureus

WINTER

Size: 6" (15 cm)

Male: Raspberry-red head, cap, breast, back and rump. Brownish wings and tail.

Female: heavily streaked brown and white bird with large white eyebrows

Juvenile: same as female

Nest: cup; female and male build; 1 brood a year

Eggs: 4-5; greenish blue with brown markings

Incubation: 12-13 days; female incubates

Fledging: 13-14 days; female and male feed young

Migration: irruptive, moves around the state in search of food

Food: seeds, insects, fruit, comes to seed feeders

Compare: Redder than the orange red of male House Finch (pg. 227), with a clear (no streaking) red breast. The male House Finch has a brown cap, compared with the male Purple Finch's red cap.

Stan's Notes: Usually only seen during the winter, when flocks of Purple Finches leave their northern homes and move around in search of food. Travels in flocks of up to 50. Comes to seed feeders along with House Finches, making it hard to tell them apart. A rich loud song and a distinctive "tic" note is made only in flight. Not a purple color, the Latin name *purpureus* means "crimson" or other reddish color.

female
pg. 237

male

SCARLET TANAGER
Piranga olivacea

Size: 7" (18 cm)

Male: Bright scarlet-red bird with jet black wings and tail. Ivory bill and dark eyes.

Female: drab greenish yellow with olive wings and tail, whitish wing linings, dark eyes

Juvenile: same as female

Nest: cup; female builds; 1 brood per year

Eggs: 4-5; blue green with brown markings

Incubation: 13-14 days; female incubates

Fledging: 9-11 days; female and male feed young

Migration: complete, to Central and South America

Food: insects, fruit

Compare: Male Summer Tanager (pg. 233) is slightly larger and rosy red in color vs. the scarlet red of the male Scarlet Tanager. Male Northern Cardinal (pg. 235) has a black mask and a red bill, and lacks the black wings of the male Scarlet Tanager.

Stan's Notes: Male sheds (molts) its bright red plumage in the fall, appearing more like the female. Prefers mature unbroken woodland, where it hunts for insects high in tops of trees. Requires a minimum of 4 acres for nesting; prefers 8 acres. Tropical-looking birds, they arrive late in spring and leave early in autumn. The Scarlet Tanager is included in some 240 tanager species in the world. Nearly all are brightly colored and live in the tropics. The name "Tanager" comes from a South American Tupi Indian word meaning "any small, brightly colored bird."

female
pg. 263

male

SUMMER TANAGER
Piranga rubra

Size: 8" (20 cm)

Male: Bright rosy-red bird with darker red wings.

Female: overall yellow with slightly darker wings

Juvenile: male has patches of red and green over the entire body, female is same as adult female

Nest: cup; female builds; 1-2 broods per year

Eggs: 3-5; pale blue with dark markings

Incubation: 10-12 days; female incubates

Fledging: unknown days; female and male feed young

Migration: complete, to Central and South America

Food: insects, fruit

Compare: Slightly larger than male Scarlet Tanager (pg. 231), which is scarlet red with black wings, compared with the rosy red of the male Summer Tanager.

Stan's Notes: Found in Kentucky where forest exists, especially in mixed pine and oak woods. Due to clearing of land for agriculture, populations have been decreasing over the past century, especially during the last two decades. Returning to Kentucky in late April and with young hatching in late May, some pairs have two broods per year. While fruit makes up some of the diet, most of it consists of insects such as bees and wasps. Summer Tanagers unfortunately seem to be parasitized by Brown-headed Cowbirds more than just about any other nesting bird in Kentucky.

female pg. 111

male

NORTHERN CARDINAL
Cardinalis cardinalis

YEAR-ROUND

Size: 8-9" (20-22.5 cm)

Male: All-red bird with a black mask extending from face down to chin and throat. Large red bill and crest.

Female: buff brown with tinges of red on crest and wings, same black mask and red bill

Juvenile: same as female, with blackish gray bill

Nest: cup; female builds; 2-3 broods per year

Eggs: 3-4; bluish white with brown markings

Incubation: 12-13 days; female and male incubate

Fledging: 9-10 days; female and male feed young

Migration: non-migrator

Food: seeds, insects, fruit, comes to seed feeders

Compare: The male Scarlet Tanager (pg. 231) has black wings and tail.

Stan's Notes: A familiar backyard bird. Look for the male feeding female during courtship. Male feeds young of the first brood by himself while female builds second nest. The name comes from the Latin word *cardinalis*, which means "important." Very territorial in spring, it will fight its own reflection in a window. Non-territorial during winter, gathering in small flocks of up to 20 birds. Both the male and female sing, and can be heard anytime of year. Listen for its "whata-cheer-cheer-cheer" territorial call in spring.

RING-BILLED GULL
Larus delawarensis

Size: 19" (48 cm)

Male: A white bird with gray wings, black wing tips spotted with white, and a white tail, as seen in flight. Yellow bill with a black ring near tip. Yellowish legs and feet. Winter or non-breeding adult has a speckled brown back of head and nape of neck.

Female: same as male

Juvenile: mostly gray version of winter adult, has a dark band at end of tail

Nest: ground; the female and male build; 1 brood per year

Eggs: 2-4; off-white with brown markings

Incubation: 20-21 days; female and male incubate

Fledging: 20-40 days; female and male feed young

Migration: complete, to southern states and Mexico

Food: insects, fish, scavenges

Compare: Similar to Herring Gull (pg. 239), which has an orange mark on tip of lower bill. Herring Gull has pink legs and feet, and lacks Ring-billed Gull's black ring.

Stan's Notes: A common gull of garbage dumps and parking lots. It is expanding its range and remains farther north longer during winter due to successful scavenging in cities. Acquires a new and different plumage in each of the first three autumns and doesn't attain adult plumage until the third year. Attains ring on bill after the first winter.

HERRING GULL
Larus argentatus

WINTER

Size: 23-26" (58-66 cm)

Male: Snow-white bird with slate gray wings and black wing tips with tiny white spots. Bill is yellow with an orange-red spot near tip of the lower bill. Pinkish legs. Winter plumage head and neck are dirty gray to brown.

Female: same as male

Juvenile: uniformly mottled brown to gray, black bill

Nest: ground; the female and male build; 1 brood per year

Eggs: 2-3; olive with brown markings

Incubation: 24-28 days; female and male incubate

Fledging: 35-36 days; female and male feed young

Migration: complete, to coasts that remain unfrozen in North America

Food: fish, insects, clams, eggs, baby birds

Compare: Larger than the Ring-billed Gull (pg. 237), which has yellowish legs and a black ring around its bill, and lacks an orange-red dot on the lower mandible.

Stan's Notes: An opportunistic bird, scavenging food from dumpsters, but will also take other birds' eggs and young right from nest. Often drops clams and other shellfish from heights to break shells and get to the soft interior. Nests in colonies, returning to same site year after year. Lines nest with grasses and seaweed. Adults molt to a dirty gray in winter, looking similar to juveniles. Takes about four years for juveniles to obtain adult plumage.

GREAT EGRET
Ardea alba

Size: 38" (96 cm)

Male: Tall, thin, elegant all-white bird with long, pointed yellow bill. Black stilt-like legs and black feet.

Female: same as male

Juvenile: same as adult

Nest: platform; male and female build; 1 brood per year

Eggs: 2-3; light blue, unmarked

Incubation: 23-26 days; female and male incubate

Fledging: 43-49 days; female and male feed young

Migration: complete, to southern states, Mexico and Central America

Food: fish, aquatic insects, frogs, crayfish

Compare: Smaller in size and similar in shape to Great Blue Heron (pg. 209).

Stan's Notes: A tall and stately bird, the Great Egret slowly stalks shallow wetlands looking for small fish to spear with its long sharp bill. Nests in colonies of up to 100 birds. Now protected, they were hunted to near extinction in the 1800s and early 1900s for their long white plumage. The name "Egret" came from the French word *aigrette*, which means "ornamental tufts of plumes." The plumes are grown near the tail during breeding season.

male pg. 221

female

AMERICAN REDSTART
Setophaga ruticilla

MIGRATION
SUMMER

Size: 5" (13 cm)

Female: Olive brown with yellow patches on sides, wings and tail. White belly.

Male: small, striking black bird with contrasting patches of orange on sides, wings and tail, white belly

Juvenile: same as female, the juvenile male is tinged orange for first year

Nest: cup; female builds; 1 brood per year

Eggs: 3-5; off-white with brown markings

Incubation: 12 days; female incubates

Fledging: 9 days; female and male feed young

Migration: complete, to Mexico, Central America and South America

Food: insects, seeds, berries rarely

Compare: Similar to female Yellow-rumped Warbler (pg. 175), but lacking the Warbler's yellow patch on rump.

Stan's Notes: A common and widespread warbler in Kentucky, mostly seen during spring migration. Prefers large unbroken tracts of forest. Appears to be hyperactive when feeding, hovering and darting back and forth to glean insects from the leaves. Look for flashing black and orange color high in the trees. Often droops its wings and fans its tail just before launching out to catch an insect.

male

winter male

female

AMERICAN GOLDFINCH
Carduelis tristis

YEAR-ROUND

Size: 5" (13 cm)

Male: A perky yellow bird with a black patch on forehead. Black tail with conspicuous white rump. Black wings with white wing bars. No marking on the chest. Dramatic change in color during winter, similar to female.

Female: dull olive yellow without a black forehead, with brown wings and a white rump

Juvenile: same as female

Nest: cup; female builds; 1 brood per year

Eggs: 4-6; pale blue, unmarked

Incubation: 10-12 days; female incubates

Fledging: 11-17 days; female and male feed young

Migration: partial migrator, flocks of up to 20 move around North America

Food: seeds, insects, will come to seed feeders

Compare: Confused with other winter birds. The Pine Siskin (pg. 75) has streaked chest and belly, and yellow wing bars. Female Purple Finch (pg. 85) has a heavily streaked chest and a white eye stripe. The female House Finch (pg. 71) has a heavily streaked white chest.

Stan's Notes: Most often found in open fields, scrubby areas and in woodland. Often called Wild Canary. A feeder bird that enjoys Nyjer thistle. Late summer nesting, uses the silky down from wild thistle for nest. Appears roller-coaster-like in flight. Listen for it to twitter during flight. Almost always in small flocks. Moves only far enough south to find food.

COMMON YELLOWTHROAT
Geothlypis trichas

Size: 5" (13 cm)

Male: Olive brown bird with bright yellow throat and breast, a white belly and a distinctive black mask outlined in white. A long, thin, pointed black bill.

Female: same as male, only lacking black mask

Juvenile: same as female

Nest: cup; female builds; 2 broods per year

Eggs: 3-5; white with brown markings

Incubation: 11-12 days; female incubates

Fledging: 10-11 days; female and male feed young

Migration: complete, to southern states and Central America

Food: insects

Compare: Found in a similar habitat as the American Goldfinch (pg. 245), but lacks the male's black forehead and wings. The male Yellow Warbler (pg. 253) has fine orange streaks on chest and lacks black mask. Yellow-rumped Warbler (pg. 175) only has spots of yellow, compared with Yellowthroat's yellow breast.

Stan's Notes: A common warbler of open fields and marshes. Has a cheerful, well-known song, "witchity-witchity-witchity-witchity." The male performs a curious courtship display, bouncing in and out of tall grass while uttering an unusual song. The young remain dependent upon the parents longer than most warblers. A frequent cowbird host.

KENTUCKY WARBLER
Oporornis formosus

Size: 5" (13 cm)

Male: Dark olive back and wings. Black cap with black extending down sides of neck. Bright yellow just above eye "spectacles." Bright yellow chin, chest and belly with the color extending underneath tail. A characteristic short tail and long legs.

Female: same as male, only black areas not as dark

Juvenile: similar to female

Nest: cup; the female and male build; 1-2 broods per year

Eggs: 3-6; white with dark markings

Incubation: 12-13 days; female incubates

Fledging: 8-10 days; female and male feed young

Migration: complete, to the Caribbean, Central and South America

Food: insects

Compare: Similar to the Magnolia Warbler (pg. 251), which has gray crown and white eyebrows instead of black cap and yellow eyebrows of the Kentucky Warbler.

Stan's Notes: One of the most common forest-dwelling birds in Kentucky, but can be very shy and usually heard more than seen. Feeds mostly on the ground, hopping along and chasing after any insects. Constructs cup nest of dead leaves, grasses and rootlets under logs or in shrubs. Can be very sensitive to deforestation. A frequent Brown-headed Cowbird host.

MAGNOLIA WARBLER
Dendroica magnolia

MIGRATION

Size: 5" (13 cm)

Male: Yellow and black warbler with a gray crown and white eyebrows. Heavy black streaks on a yellow chest and belly. White wing patch. Yellow rump. Obvious white patches on tail.

Female: similar to male, lacks black on face, has two white wing bars

Juvenile: same as female

Nest: cup; female and male build; 1 brood a year

Eggs: 3-5; white with brown markings

Incubation: 11-13 days; female incubates

Fledging: 8-10 days; female and male feed young

Migration: complete, to Central America

Food: insects

Compare: More yellow than Yellow-rumped Warbler (pg. 175). The Yellow-throated Warbler (pg. 177) has black-streaked white belly. Kentucky Warbler (pg. 249) has a black cap and yellow eyebrows. Prairie Warbler (pg. 255) has an olive back with chestnut-colored streaks.

Stan's Notes: A common warbler in Kentucky during the spring (mid-May) and fall (late August) migrations. Look for them low in trees, where they feed on insects. Often fan their tails while picking insects from the underside of leaves. Males often feed higher up in trees than females. Nests throughout Canada and the northern states. Named by chance when ornithologist Alexander Wilson spotted the bird in a magnolia tree.

male

female

YELLOW WARBLER
Dendroica petechia

MIGRATION
SUMMER

Size: 5" (13 cm)

Male: Yellow warbler with orange streaks on the chest and belly. Long, pointed dark bill.

Female: same as male, lacking orange streaking

Juvenile: similar to adult, only much duller

Nest: cup; female builds; 1 brood per year

Eggs: 4-5; white with brown markings

Incubation: 11-12 days; female incubates

Fledging: 10-12 days; female and male feed young

Migration: complete, to southern states, Mexico, and Central and South America

Food: insects

Compare: Look for orange streaking on chest of male. The male American Goldfinch (pg. 245) has black wings and forehead. The female Yellow Warbler is similar to the female American Goldfinch (pg. 245), but lacks its white wing bars.

Stan's Notes: A common warbler of gardens and shrubby areas not far from water. Males are often seen higher up in trees than the females. Females are less conspicuous. Starts to migrate south in August, returning to Kentucky in the latter part of April. Migrates at night in mixed flocks of other warblers. Rests and feeds during the day.

PRAIRIE WARBLER
Dendroica discolor

Size:	5" (13 cm)
Male:	Olive back with chestnut-colored streaks. Bright yellow from the chin to belly. Black streaks on sides from neck down. Black line through eyes. Yellow eyebrows.
Female:	same as male, only duller
Juvenile:	similar to female
Nest:	cup; female builds; 2 broods per year
Eggs:	3-5; white with brown markings
Incubation:	11-14 days; female incubates
Fledging:	8-11 days; female and male feed young
Migration:	complete, to the Caribbean
Food:	insects
Compare:	The Magnolia Warbler (pg. 251) has more black and the Yellow Warbler (pg. 253) has none. Lacks the complete black mask of the Common Yellowthroat (pg. 247). Watch for the Prairie Warbler to twitch its tail when feeding.

Stan's Notes: A common and widespread warbler in the state. Unfortunately, it was misnamed when it was first found in a barren area in Kentucky. Nests in dry, brushy clearings and forest edges, making it a perfect host for Brown-headed Cowbirds. Will sometimes desert a parasitized nest. Nests in upright fork of trees. Feeds young mainly caterpillars. Returns to Kentucky in late April to mid-May in mixed flocks of warblers.

female

male pg. 231

SCARLET TANAGER
Piranga olivacea

SUMMER

Size: 7" (18 cm)

Female: Drab greenish yellow with olive wings and tail. Whitish wing linings. Dark eyes.

Male: bright scarlet-red bird with jet black wings and tail, ivory bill and dark eyes

Juvenile: same as female

Nest: cup; female builds; 1 brood per year

Eggs: 4-5; blue green with brown markings

Incubation: 13-14 days; female incubates

Fledging: 9-11 days; female and male feed young

Migration: complete, to Central and South America

Food: insects, fruit

Compare: Slightly smaller than the female Summer Tanager (pg. 263), which is overall mustard yellow and has a larger, thicker bill. The female Baltimore Oriole (pg. 259) has gray brown wings and white wing bars.

Stan's Notes: Male sheds (molts) its bright red plumage in the fall, appearing more like the female. Prefers mature unbroken woodland, where it hunts for insects high in tops of trees. Requires a minimum of 4 acres for nesting; prefers 8 acres. Tropical-looking birds, they arrive late in spring and leave early in autumn. The Scarlet Tanager is included in some 240 tanager species in the world. Nearly all are brightly colored and live in the tropics. The name "Tanager" comes from a South American Tupi Indian word meaning "any small, brightly colored bird."

male pg. 223

female

BALTIMORE ORIOLE
Icterus galbula

Size: 7-8" (18-20 cm)

Female: A pale yellow bird with orange tones, gray brown wings, white wing bars, a gray bill and dark eyes.

Male: bright flaming-orange bird with black head and black extending down nape of neck onto the back, black wings with white and orange wing bars, an orange tail with black streaks, gray bill and dark eyes

Juvenile: same as female

Nest: pendulous; female builds; 1 brood per year

Eggs: 4-5; bluish with brown markings

Incubation: 12-14 days; female incubates

Fledging: 12-14 days; female and male feed young

Migration: complete, to Mexico, Central America and South America

Food: insects, fruit, nectar, comes to orange half and nectar feeders

Compare: Female Baltimore Oriole is often confused with the female Scarlet Tanager (pg. 257), which has olive-colored wings.

Stan's Notes: A fantastic songster, this bird is often heard before seen. Easily attracted to a feeder offering grape jelly, orange halves or sugar water (nectar). Parents bring young to feeders. Sits in tops of trees feeding on caterpillars. Female builds sock-like nest at the outermost branches of tall trees. Often returns to the same area year after year. Some of the last birds to arrive in spring (April) and first to leave in fall (August).

male pg. 225

female

ORCHARD ORIOLE
Icterus spurius

Size: 7-8" (18-20 cm)

Female: An olive green bird with a dull yellow belly. Two white wing bars on dark gray wings. Long, thin black bill with a small gray mark on lower mandible (jaw).

Male: dull orange with a black head, chin, upper back, wings and tail, single white wing bars

Juvenile: same as female, first-year male has a black bib

Nest: pendulous; female builds; 1 brood per year

Eggs: 3-5; pale blue to white, brown markings

Incubation: 11-12 days; female and male incubate

Fledging: 11-14 days; female and male feed young

Migration: complete, to central Mexico and northern South America

Food: insects, fruit, comes to fruit/nectar feeders

Compare: Similar to female Baltimore Oriole (pg. 259), which has orange overtones and more pronounced wing bars. Female Scarlet Tanager (pg. 257) has olive-colored wings.

Stan's Notes: Prefers orchards and open woods, hence its common name. Eats insects until wild fruit starts to ripen. One of the last birds to arrive in spring and one of the first to leave each fall, spending only about four to five months in Kentucky. Usually nests alone, but sometimes in small colonies. Parents bring the young to jelly and orange half feeders shortly after fledging. Many people mistakenly think the orioles have left during summer but, in fact, the birds are concentrating on finding insects to feed their young.

male pg. 233

female

SUMMER TANAGER
Piranga rubra

SUMMER

Size: 8" (20 cm)

Female: Some show a faint wash of red, but most females are a mustard yellow overall with slightly darker wings.

Male: bright rosy-red bird with darker red wings

Juvenile: male has patches of red and green over the entire body, female is same as adult female

Nest: cup; female builds; 1-2 broods per year

Eggs: 3-5; pale blue with dark markings

Incubation: 10-12 days; female incubates

Fledging: unknown days; female and male feed young

Migration: complete, to Central and South America

Food: insects, fruit

Compare: Slightly larger than female Scarlet Tanager (pg. 257), which has greenish yellow head, back and rump, compared with the yellow female Summer Tanager. Female Scarlet Tanager has darker wings than the female Summer Tanager.

Stan's Notes: Found in Kentucky where forest exists, especially in mixed pine and oak woods. Due to clearing of land for agriculture, populations have been decreasing over the past century, especially during the last two decades. Returning to Kentucky in late April and with young hatching in late May, some pairs have two broods per year. While fruit makes up some of the diet, most of it consists of insects such as bees and wasps. Summer Tanagers unfortunately seem to be parasitized by Brown-headed Cowbirds more than just about any other nesting bird in Kentucky.

male

female

EVENING GROSBEAK
Coccothraustes vespertinus

WINTER

Size: 8" (20 cm)

Male: A striking bird with a stocky body, a large ivory-to-greenish bill and bright yellow eyebrows. Dirty-yellow head, black-and-white wings and tail, and yellow rump and belly.

Female: similar to male, with softer colors, and gray head and throat

Juvenile: same as female, brown bill

Nest: cup; female builds; 1 brood per year

Eggs: 3-4; blue with brown markings

Incubation: 12-14 days; female incubates

Fledging: 13-14 days; female and male feed young

Migration: irruptive, seasonal movement brings birds to Kentucky during winter

Food: seeds, insects, fruit, comes to seed feeders

Compare: Larger than its close relative, the American Goldfinch (pg. 245). Look for the dark head with bright yellow eyebrows and the extra-large bill.

Stan's Notes: One of the largest finches. Has characteristic undulating finch-like flight. Has unusually large bill for cracking seeds, its main source of food. Often seen on gravel roads eating gravel, from which it gets minerals, salts and grit to grind up seeds it eats. Sheds the outer layer of its bill in spring, exposing blue green bill. Moves in large flocks in the winter. More numerous in some years than others.

EASTERN MEADOWLARK
Sturnella magna

YEAR-ROUND

Size: 9" (22.5 cm)

Male: A robin-shaped bird with a brown back, a lemon-yellow chest and prominent black V-shaped necklace. White outer tail feathers.

Female: same as male

Juvenile: same as adult

Nest: cup, on the ground in dense cover; female builds; 2 broods per year

Eggs: 3-5; white with brown markings

Incubation: 13-15 days; female incubates

Fledging: 11-12 days; female and male feed young

Migration: complete, to southern states and Central America

Food: insects, seeds

Compare: The only large yellow bird with a black V mark on chest.

Stan's Notes: A bird of open grassy country. Best known for its wonderful song. Often seen perched on a fence post, it will quickly dive into tall grass if approached. Has conspicuous white markings on each side of its tail, most often seen when flying away. Nest is sometimes domed with dried grass. Named "Meadowlark" because it's a bird of meadows and sings like the larks of Europe. Eastern Meadowlark's song is a flute-like, clear whistle. Not a member of the lark family, it actually belongs to the blackbird family. Related to grackles and orioles.

HELPFUL RESOURCES:

Birder's Bug Book, The. Waldbauer, Gilbert. Cambridge: Harvard University Press, 1998.

Birder's Dictionary. Cox, Randall T. Helena, MT: Falcon Press Publishing, 1996

Birder's Handbook, The. Ehrlich, Paul, David S. Dobkin and Darryl Wheye. New York: Simon and Schuster, 1988.

Birds Do It, Too: The Amazing Sex Life of Birds. Harrison, George and Kit Harrison. Minocqua, WI: Willow Creek Press, 1997.

Birds of Forest, Yard, and Thicket. Eastman, John. Mechanicsburg, PA: Stackpole Books, 1997.

Birds of North America. Kaufman, Kenn. New York: Houghton Mifflin, 2000.

Blackbirds of the Americas. Orians, Gordon H. Seattle: University of Washington Press, 1985.

Cardinal, The. Osborne, June. Austin: University of Texas Press, 1995.

Cry of the Sandhill Crane, The. Grooms, Steve. Minocqua, WI: NorthWord Press, 1992.

Dictionary of American Bird Names, The. Choate, Ernest A. Boston: Harvard Common Press, 1985.

Everything You Never Learned About Birds. Rupp, Rebecca. Pownal, VT: Storey Publishing, 1997.

Field Guide to the Birds, A: A Completely New Guide to all the Birds of Eastern and Central North America. Peterson, Roger Tory and Virginia Marie Peterson. Boston: Houghton Mifflin, 1998.

Field Guide to the Birds of North America: Third Edition. Washington, DC: National Geographic Society, 1999.

Field Guide to Warblers of North America, A. Dunn, Jon and Kimball Garrett. Boston: Houghton Mifflin, 1997.

Folklore of Birds. Martin, Laura C. Old Saybrook, CT: Globe Pequot Press, 1993

Guide to Bird Behavior, A: Vol I, II, III. Stokes, Donald and Lillian Stokes. Boston: Little, Brown and Company, 1989.

How Birds Migrate. Kerlinger, Paul. Mechanicsburg, PA: Stackpole Books, 1995

Kentucky Breeding Bird Atlas, The. Palmer-Ball, Brainard, Jr. Lexington: University Press of Kentucky, 1996.

Lives of Birds, The: Birds of the World and Their Behavior. Short, Lester L. Collingdale, PA: DIANE Publishing, 2000.

Lives of North American Birds. Kaufman, Kenn. Boston: Houghton Mifflin, 1996

Living on the Wind. Weidensaul, Scott. New York: North Point Press, 2000.

National Audubon Society: North American Birdfeeder Handbook. Burton, Robert. New York: Dorling Kindersley Publishing, 1995.

National Audubon Society: The Sibley Guide to Birds. Sibley, David Allen. New York: Alfred A. Knopf, 2000.

Photographic Guide to North American Raptors, A. Wheeler, Brian K. and William S. Clark. New York: Academic Press, 1999.

Secret Lives of Birds, The. Gingras, Pierre. Toronto: Key Porter Books, 1997.

Secrets of the Nest. Dunning, Joan. Boston: Houghton Mifflin, 1994.

Sparrows and Buntings: A Guide to the Sparrows and Buntings of North America and the World. Byers, Clive, Jon Curson and Urban Olsson. New York: Houghton Mifflin, 1995.

Stokes Bluebird Book: The Complete Guide to Attracting Bluebirds. Stokes, Donald and Lillian Stokes. Boston: Little, Brown and Company, 1991.

Stokes Field Guide to Birds: Eastern Region. Stokes, Donald and Lillian Stokes. Boston: Little, Brown and Company, 1996.

Stokes Purple Martin Book. Stokes, Donald and Lillian Stokes. Boston: Little, Brown and Company, 1997.

KENTUCKY BIRDING HOTLINES:

To report unusual bird sightings or possibly hear recordings of where birds have been seen, you can often call pre-recorded hotlines detailing such information. Since these hotlines are usually staffed by volunteers, and phone numbers and even the organizations that host them often change, the phone numbers are not listed here. To obtain the numbers, go to your favorite internet search engine, type in something like "rare bird alert hotline Kentucky" and follow the links provided.

WEB PAGES:

The internet is a valuable place to learn more about birds. You may find birding on the net a fun way to discover additional information or to spend a long winter night. These web sites will assist you in your pursuit of birds. If a web address doesn't work (they often change a bit), just enter the name of the group into a search engine to track down the new address.

SITE	ADDRESS
Kentucky Ornithological Society	www.biology.eku.edu/kos.htm
American Birding Association	www.americanbirding.org
Cornell Lab of Ornithology	www.birds.cornell.edu
Author Stan Tekiela's home page	www.naturesmart.com

ABOUT THE AUTHOR:

Naturalist, wildlife photographer and writer Stan Tekiela is the originator of the popular state-specific field guides such as *Birds of West Virginia Field Guide*. For over two decades, Stan has authored more than 100 field guides, nature appreciation books and wildlife audio CDs for nearly every state in the nation, presenting many species of birds, mammals, reptiles and amphibians, trees, wildflowers and cacti. Holding a Bachelor of Science degree in Natural History from the University of Minnesota and as an active professional naturalist for more than 20 years, Stan studies and photographs wildlife throughout the United States and has received various national and regional awards for his books and photographs. Also a well-known columnist and radio personality, his syndicated column appears in over 20 newspapers and his wildlife programs are broadcast on a number of Midwest radio stations. He is a member of the North American Nature Photography Association and Canon Professional Services. Stan resides in Victoria, Minnesota, with his wife, Katherine, and daughter, Abigail. He can be contacted via his web page at www.naturesmart.com.